# STRESS-FREE
# MOTORBOATING

Duncan Wells

# STRESS-FREE
# MOTORBOATING

## SINGLE AND SHORT-HANDED TECHNIQUES

ADLARD
COLES

LONDON • OXFORD • NEW YORK • NEW DELHI • SYDNEY

*To the girls – Sally, Katie and Ellie*

ADLARD COLES
Bloomsbury Publishing Plc
50 Bedford Square, London, WC1B 3DP
29 Earlsfort Terrace, Dublin 2, Ireland

BLOOMSBURY, ADLARD COLES and the Buoy logo are trademarks of
Bloomsbury Publishing Plc

This edition first published 2017

Copyright Duncan Wells © 2017

Duncan Wells has asserted his right under the Copyright, Designs and
Patents Act, 1988, to be identified as Author of this work

British Library Cataloguing-in-Publication Data
A catalogue record for this book is available from the British Library

Library of Congress Cataloguing-in-Publication data has been applied for

ISBN: PB:   978-1-4729-2782-8
       ePDF: 978-1-4729-4730-7
       ePub: 978-1-4729-4729-1

4  6  8  10  9  7  5

Designed and typeset in 10.5 on 13pt Bliss Light by Susan McIntyre
Printed and bound in India by Replika Press Pvt. Ltd.

To find out more about our authors and books visit www.bloomsbury.com.
and sign up for our newsletters

All photographs were taken by or on behalf of Duncan Wells, except that
of the *Souris-Rose*, page 115, by Jill Kempthorne-Ley.
Synoptic chart on page 127 © British Crown Copyright 2013. Used under
licence from the Met Office.
Screenshots on page 136 courtesy of iNavx App and Traverse.com.

# CONTENTS

# ACKNOWLEDGEMENTS

I would like to thank all those who lent support, advice, boats and enthusiasm, without which this book would not have been possible.

So thank you to:

- David and Jo-Ann Ramos and *Ramosseas*, their Sealine F42.
- Becki Gravestock, for introducing me to them and for being wonderful. She also features in the MOB Lifesavers videos.
- Andy and Gale Mold, Holly the dog and *Hollywood*, their Pearl 60.
- Les and Carol Squires and their Fairline 42, *Slip Knot*.
- John and Åsa Curzon and their Princess 52, *Ivy Sea*, for showing me so many neat ideas for making things simple and safe when it comes to mooring.
- Derek Withrington from SeaSmart Marine, for giving me the lowdown on smelly heads.
- Tim Griffin from Griffin Marine Services, for advice on launching (and recovering) boats from (and to) trailers.
- My great friends Andrew and Kay Rogers, for their patience and help with *Katcha*, their Broom 29.

- Roy May and Bisham Abbey Sailing and Navigation School, for the single-handing masterclass on Roy's 17m barge, *Le Coq*.
- Simon and Caroline Newell, for always being there and making their Doral Boca Grande 44, *Evelyn*, available at every opportunity. We certainly discovered some things, particularly in the man-overboard retrieval stakes.
- Alan Mainstone, for letting me try some interesting single-handing stuff with his 28ft Aquador, *Freedom*.
- Andy Hobbs, for letting me hold his 23m Princess, *Lucky Ash*, on to the dock by driving against just one stern line. I checked the cleats on shore and on board and the line before I clicked the 1350hp engine into gear!
- Martyn Whitwell and President Wensleydale for excellent narrowboat single-handing and for agreeing to appear on the cover.
- David and Karen Starkey and their Aquastar 43 *Kapana IV*.
- And finally on a boat front, Jonathan and Rebecca Parker and their Bavaria 32, *Tanzanite*.

Jonathan is the Operations Manager of Sea Start – AA for the sea – and his knowledge of boats and engines, and what they do and what they don't do, is limitless. We met at a low point in my boating life when I had run out of fuel. Of course, I convinced everyone that there was something wrong with the engine. We *couldn't* have run out of fuel – I had records to show that there was fuel in the tank. No, there must be a fuel blockage. This had the experts, including Jonathan, flummoxed. Air in the system meant no fuel in the tank.

'No,' I said. 'There has to be fuel in the tank, otherwise I've lost 80 litres and that's quite a bit to lose – you'd smell it, you'd think.' I was persuasive: there *must* be a blockage. I even got an engineer to fit a new fuel pump. The whole exercise cost me a lot of money.

Then I checked the 80-litre reserve tank, which of course had to be empty. Only ... it was full. Ah, so that was where the 80 litres were – exactly where they should have been. And I hadn't dropped the reserve into the main tank, as I had thought, so the main tank was empty, just as Jonathan had said. *Oeuf sur le visage.*

Moral of the story? Never listen to the owner or skipper on matters of fuel. *Always* dip the tank.

Thank you to Janet Murphy at Adlard Coles for the commission and for believing in me, and thank you, of course, to Penny Phillips, a like-minded soul who edited *Stress-Free Motorboating* with a firm but fair hand and helped to produce a better product than I delivered to her. You will notice she has allowed that sentence to remain. [Oh, yeah? Not without editing it with a firm but fair hand, she hasn't!]

Of course, there were many other friends who held cameras, proffered hands for this or that knot, or allowed me to board their boats to take shots. Pete and Lorna Lovett: thanks for letting me board *Namaste* for shots of string and so forth.

Thanks to Ellie for all her help on MOB retrieval.

Finally, as ever, thanks to my family for allowing me the time to go out on the water and find these things out.

# PREFACE

This book is very different from any other motorboating book you will have come across. *Stress-Free Motorboating* takes the business of boat handling by just one or two people and focuses on groundbreaking ways of making things simpler and easier to manage: getting on and off berths, picking up and dropping mooring buoys, anchoring. Also presented here is the answer to man-overboard retrieval, MOB Lifesavers (www.moblifesavers.com), including video links to show some of the described techniques in action.

Throughout the book you will see a symbol like this ▌ and the words 'Scan the QR code to watch a video on ...'. If you have a smartphone or tablet and a quick response (QR) code-reader app (which you can download free), you scan the QR code and the video will play on your device. If you don't have a phone or tablet, you can go to westviewsailing.co.uk/stress-free-mboating and view the videos there.

Motorboats are incredibly expensive to buy and to run, and many people come to them after the first flush of youth has passed them by. Some people who have been sailors all their lives 'retire' to motorboating. So some crews are not as athletic as they might be, and short-handed techniques that allow them to manage their boat from the cockpit are required. At the same time, young people new to boating will also benefit from adopting the short-handed techniques suggested in this book.

I have spent a lot of time with owners of various motorboats, discussing issues they have and finding answers both with them and for them. I have looked at all the things needed to manage a boat, and have broken these down into steps and tried to find ways of making them easier.

Apart from writing books and articles for the yachting press, I am also the principal of Westview Sailing. We leave the practical courses to others, but we teach the shore-based theory courses and offer video tutorials, which cover all the shore-based navigational disciplines. RYA students find these very useful as study aids (www.westviewsailing.co.uk/video tutorials). If you want to take the tutorials out on the water with you, please download them from Udemy.

Finally – and I have borrowed this from Eric Hiscock, doyen of the sail cruising world – in relation to the fairer sex: I know you invariably to be quicker to learn than us chaps and just as skilful in the art of navigation and sailing, and that you don't make as much fuss about everything as we do, so I am sure you will understand that when I say 'he', I mean 'she' equally. Thus an MOB, man overboard, can be as much a woman – or indeed a child – as a man.

I hope you enjoy the book and find the techniques useful. I use them every time I go out on the water. If you have any ideas you'd like to share, or improvements on what I suggest, please do not hesitate to contact me.

# 1 INTRODUCTION AND PHILOSOPHY

I had my RYA Day Skipper theory. I had my Day Skipper practical. And now I had 45 feet of Princess motorboat ... well, 53, actually, if you measured the way berthing masters do, from the tip of the anchor on the bow to the end of the dinghy hanging off the davits at the back – er, sorry, stern.

The man who sold it to me, Bernard, hadn't really wanted to sell it at all. He'd been persuaded by the marina to upgrade and had been told they would sell it for him. After six months and no bites, he called the marina sales office asking for a boat with exactly the specification of his boat (which they were meant to be selling): 'with reverse-cycle air-conditioning and a dinghy, say 3 metres, with a beefy outboard, say 30hp?' 'I'm sorry, sir – we haven't got anything like that.'

Well, that was it – red rag to a bull. Bernard would show them how to market a boat! And he did. I read the ad in *Motor Boat & Yachting* magazine and called the number straight away. I had been looking for two years at all available Princess 45s because I knew that was the boat I wanted to buy, and having ticked them all off the list I knew all the boats that were available. This was a new one to me.

It was only after I had made the call that I noticed Bernard's STD code was the same as mine: he actually lived just a couple of miles down the road. I told him that if the boat was what he said it was, in the condition stated, I would buy it. Bernard took this with a pinch of salt. He'd had boats all his life, knew the business, knew what punters were like, and this was just another cock-and-bull line from a fender-kicker. He doubted very much that he would hear from me again.

Two months later, after an engine check and a sea trial and with the banker's draft in his hand, Bernard

realised I was serious. I earned a lot of brownie points in Bernard's eyes for honouring the commitment and seeing the deal through. It wasn't hard: the boat was exactly as he had described.

Bernard stood there a moment. 'Well, goodbye, then.' He stepped off the boat and headed down the dock.

I took stock of the situation. This boat had mains power, a 12-volt system and a 24-volt system. I hadn't a clue how any of that worked. What if it went wrong? Come to that, how did you drive this boat?

Bernard was making his way somewhat dejectedly to the gate.

'Bernard, Bernard!' I chased after him. 'Er, you haven't got another boat yet, have you? How would you like to stay with *Abraxas*? Show me the ropes and so forth?'

'Delighted, old boy.'

And that is how Bernard became a friend and taught me how to look after a boat and how to be a boat owner. In fact, Bernard helped me to sell *Abraxas* to the next owner. Bernard continued to stay with *Abraxas*, and this new owner also became a friend. When the time came, Bernard helped *him* to sell the boat, too. But this time, it went out of the 'family' and disappeared off over the horizon. (Well, to Brighton, at least.)

The point is that you do your RYA courses, and these are very necessary, but until you are in charge of a boat you don't really start to learn what it's all about. And often you might take your family out when you are newly 'qualified' and frighten both them and yourself. Everyone has to learn, of course, but if you can master a few techniques that make handling the boat easier, and if you can understand what the boat is likely to do in a given situation, you can build confidence so that when

you take the family out they are less anxious – in fact, they enjoy it and want to come back for more.

A lot of the time, apart from gaining experience in handling the boat and practising the manoeuvres you need to master – getting off the dock, getting back on, anchoring, picking up mooring buoys and so on – it is a question of not biting off more than you can chew.

You need to be in tune with the weather, to appreciate that wind over tide (wind against tide) will shorten the sea and give you quite an unpleasant ride, whereas wind with tide will flatten out the sea and give you a smooth ride. At sea you need to know how conditions might alter throughout the time you are out on the water. Wind strengths vary. The wind might strengthen during the day. It might change direction: a gradient wind (that is, the forecast wind) from the south may change to a northerly wind as the sea breeze kicks in.

A wind strength of Force 4 (up to 16 knots) may be as much wind as you might want for a comfortable day. At Force 5 (up to 21 knots), everything becomes a little more serious. Windage on the boat means that at low speeds when berthing, you will be blown around a great deal more. The wind on the water will start to create white crests, and wave heights will be increased. So you need to establish what weather you and your family are comfortable with. And you need to keep a beady eye on the forecast and go out only when things are just right.

On a river, you need to make sure the current is not running faster than you can handle.

When seeking a route to stress-free motorboating I always ask, 'What troubles you about boating? What manoeuvre gets your heart going?' Invariably I find the answer will involve attaching the boat to something or detaching it from something, whether the dock or a mooring buoy. Anchoring can get people excited, too.

In *Stress-Free Motorboating* I have looked at everything from the point of view of the short-handed sailor – a couple. Almost always the physically weaker partner will take on the duty of the crew, while the stronger will be on the helm. I like couples to try to reverse this where possible, but often if there's a woman in the relationship she may not want the responsibility of being in charge of the ship. Where she does, I welcome this. The groundbreaking techniques I propose take strength into account.

It is quite possible to single-hand certain boats (narrowboats, barges and some of the smaller motorboats), but getting up and down to a flybridge on the generally steep steps – sometimes effectively no more than a ladder – is not easy.

It's all very well to suggest the use of extending boathooks that crew can use to place a line around a cleat from on board, but quite often this extended boathook is pretty heavy. I am never keen on anyone stepping off until a boat is stopped and attached to the dock, so I am a great believer in getting rope to help. A length of rope will very often make things a lot easier. For mooring, you can remain on the boat and lasso the cleat, and this is something you can practise. With the cleat lassoed, the helm can drive the boat against this to hold it alongside. Or the helm can 'blip' the engines and thrusters, while the crew attaches the bow line, preferably from on board.

There are devices you can use – such as Hook & Moor and Moorfast – and if these work for you, that's fine. I like to look at more robust and more general-purpose techniques using rope.

Whatever you do, a priority should be to make things as easy as possible. And, of course, you need to prepare for the job. So much of boating is a matter of planning, preparing and anticipation:

## Planning, preparing and anticipation

**Planning** is pretty straightforward. This covers everything you do before getting on the boat. You decide where you are going and you consider the state of the weather, the tide, the river – wherever you happen to be.

**Preparing** is the real key to making sure that everything will run smoothly. Having a line ready, led the right way (under or over the guardrail, depending on the circumstances), to lasso a cleat, bollard or buoy, or to hand to a lock-keeper is preparation. Not having the line ready means the helm will have to hold the boat on station while you sort out a line. The wind may be blowing the boat, the helm may not be able to control this and things may become awkward – simply because the line was not ready. And communication between skipper and crew is an important part of preparation. If both are briefed about what is expected of them, everything will go much more smoothly. Having handy and practised techniques for things is essential for reducing any stress in boating.

**Anticipation** comes in two parts. First, anticipation derives from understanding how your boat will behave in any given circumstance: how it handles and what effect the wind, tide or stream will have. Anticipation also comes from experience. If you're faced with a new situation, what is likely to happen?

What's the one thing that gets everyone going? Correct, mooring … getting off and then back on to the dock. And these manoeuvres are performed in public, of course. You wouldn't think so to look at the marina: there is not a soul about as you prepare to depart. But make a cock-up of it and heads will pop up all around. People will emerge from companionways, fender in hand, desperate to protect their precious boats from the marauding danger that is you. Others will be watching from behind their smoked-glass saloon windows. You can't see in – but they can sure see out. So, lesson one: no shouting, no raised voices, no over-revving of the engine, no furious bow-thrusting.

The boats we used were:
*   **Princess 52** *Ivy Sea*
    Flybridge, twin engines, shaft drives, bow and stern thruster
*   **Aquador 28C** *Freedom*
    Cabin cruiser, single engine, stern drive
*   **Bavaria 32** *Tanzanite*
    Sports cruiser, twin engines, stern drives, bow thruster
*   **Doral 44 Boca Grande** *Evelyn*
    Sports cruiser, twin engines, stern drives, bow thruster
*   **Fairline Squadron 44** *Slip Knot*
    Flybridge, twin engines, shaft drive, bow thruster
*   **Barge 17m** *Le Coq*
    Single engine
*   **Broom 29** *Katcha*
    Cabin cruiser, single engine, shaft drive, bow thruster
*   **Sealine F42** *Ramosseas*
    Flybridge, twin engines, pod drive
*   **Pearl 60** *Hollywood*
    Flybridge, twin engines, shaft drives, bow and stern thruster
*   **Princess 23M** *Lucky Ash*
    Flybridge, twin engines, shaft drives, bow and stern thruster
*   **Aqua Star 46** *Kapana IV*
    Semi-displacement cruiser, shaft drives, bow thruster

The boats that joined in: left to right from top left, *Freedom, Kapana IV, Katcha, Ramosseas, Tanzanite, Le Coq, Ivy Sea, Lucky Ash, Hollywood, Evelyn, Slip Knot.*

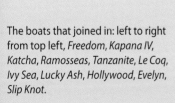

# 2 SKILLS AND DISCIPLINES

To run your boat efficiently and to manage either single-handed or short-handed you need a number of skills and handy shortcuts under the belt that will make life that bit easier.

Let's start with rope.

## ROPE

Rope is used for mooring lines, for fender lines, for painters on the bow of the dinghy and sometimes for anchor cables. I am also going to advocate the use of rope to make things easier for yourself: for getting on to and off the dock and for picking up mooring buoys. The boathook is handy for this as well, but a combination of boathook and rope can make possible what seems like the impossible (see Chapter 8).

There are really only two types of rope: those that float and those that don't. Beyond that, the differences in rope relate to its ability to stretch or not. Mooring up with rope that has no stretch at all on a windy night could cause a very jerky night's sleep. Rope with some give would make for a more comfortable night.

Here are some ropes that you will be familiar with. Plus one that you may not associate with motorboating:

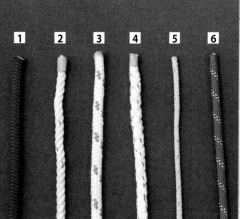

▲
1. Polyester braid dock line.
2. Polyester three-strand dock line.
3. Polyester core and braid outer.
4. Nylon multiplait.
5. Polypropylene.
6. Dyneema core in a polyester braid outer.

### Ropes at a glance

| Name | Stretch | Used for | U/V rating | Sinks/floats |
|---|---|---|---|---|
| Polyester braid stretch weave | High | Mooring warps | 5 | Sinks |
| Polyester three-strand | Low | Mooring warps | 5 | Sinks |
| Polyester core and polyester braid outer | Low | Warps and generally about the boat | 4 | Sinks |
| Nylon muliplait | Very high | Anchor cable and mooring warps | 4 | Sinks slowly |
| Polypropylene | Low | Safety and sports gear | 2 | Floats |
| Dyneema | Very low | Sheets, halyards and safety gear | 5 | Raw Dyneema floats but will sink when in a polyester braid outer |

UV rating: 5 degrades slowly, 1 degrades quickly

I have introduced Dyneema, which is an ultra high molecular weight polyethylene (HMPE) rope, because it is very light and very strong. It will be used to retrieve an MOB in Chapter 13.

And here's my first tip for stress-free motorboating. On the bigger boats the length of the mooring lines is so great and their gauge so wide that when you come to coil them they are unwieldy and weigh a great deal more than you want to handle. I can't imagine what it is like for someone not quite as beefy as me to be tasked with this job.

## Moor with Dyneema warps

Purists will use four lines for mooring up, but most people will use just two, and the line that doubles up as both bowline and back spring is naturally very long indeed on a large boat. Let's lighten this load.

When you moor up, instead of using the heavy, long polyester lines, or warps as they are called, use thinner-gauge Dyneema: 20mm polyester has the same breaking strain as 12mm Dyneema. So now you have a set of lines for arriving at the dock that are light, easy to handle and very strong.

Once moored, you can replace these with the traditional heavier, stretched polyester lines. Although

I recommend seeing whether the lighter Dyneema lines give you a quiet night.

## Buy really good quality

You have to use rope about the boat, so you might as well have rope that is comfortable to work with. I don't want to get rope burns every time I try to coil a rough line. Good-quality, comfortable rope will make an enormous difference to the way the crew feel about doing their job. They deserve the best. Give them the best.

## Use the right rope for the job

Does the rope need to be stretchy or not? Safety products need floating polypropylene. Mooring warps don't need to float but might need to stretch and be hard-wearing. A short line used as a snubber for the anchor chain to take the strain off the windlass will not need to be nice new rope but could be a short length of old nylon three-strand. Any rope to be rove through blocks for any lifting tackle to be suspended from davits will need to be high-quality braid to keep friction in the system to a minimum.

▲ Heavy mooring warps.

▲ Dyneema line, much lighter.

▲ A 60ft boat moored with Dyneema lines.

## Look after your rope

Hang it up to dry. Wet rope doesn't dry quickly when laid flat in a locker, it just makes the locker damp.

Put your rope into a pillow case, tie it tight with a bit of string and put it into the washing machine with a little fabric softener. Then it will be smooth to the touch and smell nice. Don't leave rope in foredeck lockers where it can get wet or near petrol and oil cans where any leakage can ruin it.

▶ Lines hanging up to dry.

### Use the right length of line

If you're going to lasso a cleat by the bathing platform every time you come into your berth, you don't want a long line. Have a shorter line made up for this. Choose a rope that has some body to it, perhaps a polyester core with a polyester braid outer or a polyester three-strand.

If you single-hand a narrowboat you may want a very long line to run from the cockpit to the bow, on to the shore and back to the cockpit and just a short line for the stern. Make sure you have these made up to your requirements.

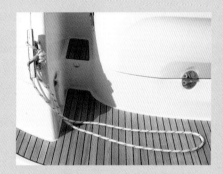

▲ Short looped line ready to drop over a cleat on shore.

▶ The helm can drive against this line to hold the boat alongside.

▲ A long line for the bow and a short line for the stern on a narrowboat allow the skipper to single-hand through locks.

# Coiling a line

There are a couple of ways of coiling a line (the sailor's way and the climber's way) and several ways of finishing them off (the sailor's way, the navy way and the gasket coil hitch). The idea is to end up with a tidy coil that will unravel nicely without tangling.

### Coiling a line the sailor's way

Start with any eye splice or any other loop that may be in the rope. You want this on the inside and the free end to be available for finishing off the coil. Make the coils at least as long as in the pictures to the right. All rope needs to be coiled clockwise, whether it be braid or three-strand. If you coil against the twist of the stranding then you're in danger of opening out the rope. When the rope is coiled correctly it feels right, natural and relaxed and it will hang in nice loops.

To help three-strand lie nicely you need to give a little twist, a half turn of the hand, as you make each loop. With stranded rope you can feel that it wants to do this, so go with the direction of the twist.

### Coiling a line the climber's way

The first coil goes into the hand and the second coil goes between the thumb and forefinger. As you keep doing this you are getting loops of line on either side.

### Finishing the coil

It doesn't matter which way you coil the line but always leave some rope available for the finish and take a few turns or wraps round the coils.

▲ Start with the eye splice on the inside of the coil.

Now it is a question of how to finish off. Here are three options:

**1 The navy way.** The simplest of all and good for hanging up a rope but not so good for laying down in a locker as it can come undone. Take the running end of the rope above the top wrap and through the coils. Done.

**2 The sailor's way.** Take a bight/loop of rope through the coils and

▲ Coiling a line the climber's way.

▲ Coil the rope clockwise, keeping even loops.

then take the running end, the loose end, through this. This is ideal for hanging the rope up. It will also be fine lying flat in a locker.

**3 The gasket coil hitch.** Take a bight of rope through the coils and over the top. Pull down and tighten. This is ideal for stowing ropes flat in a locker as the 'hitch' generally does not come loose or undone.

▲ Three ways to finish a rope: gasket coil hitch, sailor's way, navy way. Note how the gasket coil hitch does not hang nicely.

▲ Finishing a coil the sailor's way.

▲ Take a bight through the coils…

▲ over the top of the coils…

▲ then pull down and tighten.

▲ That won't come undone in the locker.

 Scan this QR code to watch a video on coiling a rope the sailor's way and the climber's way and the three finishes:

**TOP TIP**

When you are coiling braided rope you'll find that it often forms itself naturally into a figure of eight. Don't fight this, just let it happen if that's what the rope wants to do.

▶ Finishing a coil the navy way.

## Tidying up spare line

If you have a good deal of line/ mooring warp left over you can tidy this in a number of ways. You can cheese it, wrap it over the guard rail or hang it up.

Cheesing is very pretty, but any line lying on the deck for any length of time will get wet and collect dirt. I always think cheesing belongs to the superyacht brigade with crew who spend their time permanently washing and polishing things. Wrapping the line over the rail works fine, as does hanging it up, although a wrap never undoes nicely. Where a coil can be flaked out neatly, I always find that a wrap requires me to start from scratch.

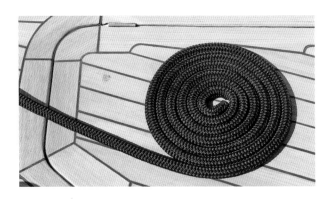

▶ Cheesed.

▲ Wrapped.

▲ Hung.

## ATTACHING TO THE DOCK

Where a line has a pre-spliced eye, keep this on board, always. It is always the free end that goes on to the dock. This is a key part of being prepared.

All lines must be free to run; a line with a pre-spliced eye in it or a loop will catch on something as you bring it back on board – guaranteed. So eyes and loops stay on board.

Even the free end of a line can wrap itself around a shoreside cleat alarmingly fast if you haul it in too quickly or, worse, try to flip it off a cleat. Flipping never works when you want it to. So rather than try to flip a line off, always set it to slip and just haul in steadily. If you are ever running bridles or slipped lines and a certain amount of line will be passing across the deck, make sure you keep the decks clear, with as few opportunities for the line to snag as possible.

### KNOTS vs. SPLICES

Knots weaken rope much more than a splice. If you put a knot in a piece of rope you weaken it considerably. A bowline tied into the end of a line will reduce its strength by 40%. But if you splice an eye into the end of the line you weaken it by only 10%.

So you attach the pre-spliced eye to the on-board cleat. This is the standing end of the line. If you don't have eyes in the ends of your mooring lines or warps, you can make a loop by tying a bowline. Or you can OXO the line on to the on-board cleat.

## OXO

This method really does work. It saves a lot of fuss and it looks neat. If you OXO every time, you know where you are.

An OXO will not undo, it will not tighten on itself over time and it can be undone under load. Of course, you want to feel comfortable that you've left your pride and joy safe, so adding in a hitch is perfectly acceptable, but you don't need it – the OXO will be perfectly secure without it with most types of rope. The only exceptions might be some polyester braids or braid outers such as those that cover Dyneema, which can slip and usually benefit from a hitch on the end of the OXO. If you're going to add a hitch, tie it so it lies down with the lay of the rope on the top of the OXO. This is the seamanlike way.

▲ Eye splice stays on board.

▲ Eye through the centre of the cleat, if it has a centre.

▲ The eye of the warp goes over each wing of the cleat.

▲ Here a bowline is tied in the end of the line to make a loop.

▲ Lead the line around the cleat.

▲ Make a complete turn around the cleat: O.

▲ Cross over to make the first half of the X.

▲ And again to complete the X.

▲ Finish with another complete turn around the cleat for the second O.

▲ Adding in an extra hitch to the OXO.

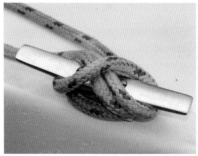

▲ A hitch has been added to the second part of the X in this variant of the OXO.

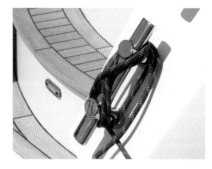

▲ Polyester braid outer requiring a hitch to secure.

I am told that an OXO can tighten itself from the bottom up if you have a very big boat straining at its warps as it is moved by the tide. And you may find that a hitch has seized. I have never experienced this, not having owned a big enough boat, but this is why large boats never ever use hitches to finish off their OXOs. Crew on big ships will just take another O around the cleat. Quite often, instead of the second O, a hitch is added with the second part of the X. This looks very neat and I have never known it to fail.

 Scan this QR code to watch a video on OXOing a line around a cleat:

## Mooring lines

You need a bow line, stern line and two springs: a head spring (forward spring, bow spring) to stop the bow moving forward and a back spring (aft spring, stern spring) to stop the stern moving backwards. Some will use one line for each of these 'jobs', and some use four lines.

This makes a great deal of sense on a large boat where long, heavy mooring warps can be quite difficult to manage. In practice, most people will use one line from the bow to shore and then bring this up to a midship cleat as the back spring and then one line from the stern to the shore and up to the same midship cleat for the head spring, all tied off with an OXO and not a bird's nest in sight.

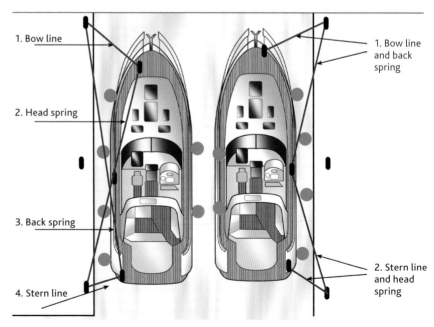

1. Bow line
2. Head spring
3. Back spring
4. Stern line

1. Bow line and back spring
2. Stern line and head spring

▲ Mooring lines.

Some will also use rubber snubbers on their lines. I have never thought much of them – they're unsightly for a start – and the way mooring line is made today, with a loose weave polyester to allow stretch, there is plenty of give to prevent boats snatching at their moorings.

## Slipped lines

You'll use slipped lines a great deal. Three points to be aware of with slipped lines:

* Ensure the amount of line you are hauling in, the free end, is as short as possible.

* Ensure there is nothing for the line to snag on when you haul it in.

* Lead the line carefully so that the two parts of the line, the outboard part and the inboard part, will not rub on each other as you haul in on the inboard end.

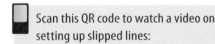  Scan this QR code to watch a video on setting up slipped lines:

## Hauling in a boat on the end of a line

It really is extremely important to get a line under a cleat to get any purchase on it. We have all seen crew crouched in the waterski position trying to haul in a very heavy boat against a fair old breeze and a wicked tide – although with thrusters and engines, the helm should be more than able to hold the boat alongside the dock. But if the crew do need to assist, the key is to get the line under a cleat, to get some purchase. Or if there is significant strain, under one wing of the cleat and over the other. Then, to bring the boat in, haul on the line using your body weight and take up the slack. Do this bit by bit until the boat is alongside.

▲ Get the line under a cleat.

▲ Under one wing and over the other for added purchase.

▲ Use the weight of your body to haul the boat in, rather than muscle power. I have lots of weight and have to lean back only slightly for this big chap to come alongside.

▲ The crew probably need a week's notice to get this off!

## Mooring to tidal quays

Set lines that are four times the range of the tide in length to allow you to rise and fall with the tide. Generally I set slipped lines so that I can control things from the boat. If I have not allowed enough line, then, as the boat falls, I can ease out a bit more. If I tie my lines to the dock, the boat may fall with the tide to a point where it is no longer possible to reach up or climb up to the dock to release the line in the event that I want to leave.

## The lasso

To be able to lasso a cleat or a mooring buoy first time every time is to have a valuable skill in your armoury. Practice, of course, is important, but using the right kind of line is key.

As we have discovered, the only ropes on board generally tend to be the mooring warps. These can be anything from some fairly mouldy three-strand to the latest sexy polyester-braid, stretchable mooring warps, neither of which is ideal for lassoing. The loose-weave polyester braid tends to flop and the three-strand, if it is old, will tend to be too stiff.

Now's the chance to invest in some rope that will be used just for lassoing. Polyester core in a polyester braid outer is nice. A polyester three-strand works well, too. You need a rope with a little weight to it, not floppy, but not too stiff. And you always need a line that is long enough for the job.

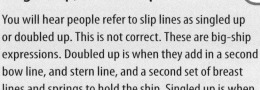

### Singled up, doubled up

You will hear people refer to slip lines as singled up or doubled up. This is not correct. These are big-ship expressions. Doubled up is when they add in a second bow line, and stern line, and a second set of breast lines and springs to hold the ship. Singled up is when they get rid of the extra lines and lie to just one bow and stern line and one set of breast lines and springs.

In fact, the call from the captain, prior to departure, is often to 'single up to springs', meaning that they will lie to just the one set of spring lines. So if you want the crew to run the lines to the shore and back to the boat ready to be released from on board, the instruction should be: 'Make the lines ready to slip, please.' 'Please' always goes down well with crew!

I have heard that on rivers when you take a turn round a bollard or a palm head, this is referred to as doubling up, and that is a matter of local context. For me, a line from the boat to the shore and back to the boat ready to release is a line set to slip.

▲ Nice rope for lassoing: polyester core in a polyester braid outer.

Then you need to make one end of the line fast to the boat. This end is known as the standing end.

Next, flake the line so there are no twists in it. Flaking means you lay down first that which you require last.

Now at the end of the rope (the running end), make four even coils. You don't want great long loops for the coils; coils a foot across will do it for me. Make sure that you have made these coils sufficiently far along the line from the standing end, where the line is attached to the boat, so as not to impair 'swing' or 'flick'.

Having made the four coils, divide them in two and hold one half of the coils in one hand, with the other half in the other hand. Make sure the two halves are joined by just one part of the line. Now, holding on to the end of the line by tucking it under your third finger and little finger, hold the coils high and then flick them high and wide at what you wish to lasso.

You don't generally have much room for a swing and tend to have to throw the line with a flick of the wrist. If holding the running end of the line and flicking at the same time is tricky, then, assuming the line is long enough, tie the running end off on a cleat on board. Now your lasso line is a loop and there is no danger of losing 'the end'.

When the rope has landed on the dock, resist the temptation to pull it in quickly as this can make it miss or jump over the cleat you are trying to secure. Haul it in steadily, making sure it catches on the wings of the cleat. If you're lassoing from above you need to make sure you don't lift the line off the wings of the cleat, so care must be taken.

 Scan the QR code for a video on lassoing:

## Throwing a line

In my experience, a line thrown to someone often does not get there first time. It always gets there second time. Why? Because when it missed first time it went into the drink and for the second throw the line is now wet. It weighs more and it goes further. One way to make it get there first time every time is to throw the line beyond what or who you're aiming at and then it is guaranteed to make the distance.

▲ Coils joined by just one part of the line.

▲ Jonathan has thrown the coils high and wide and has landed the lasso well beyond the cleat he has aimed for.

▲ A nice solid and successful lasso.

# KNOTS

You need only a couple of knots to make life a breeze. Wonderful videos and graphics on how to tie all knots can be found on the internet. I describe here only those for which I have a fondness or a handy way to remember them.

## Bowline

The knot you will probably use most during your boating life, the bowline forms a secure loop at the end of a line. It will not undo when under tension, but it does not jam, and when not under tension you can break the back of the knot to undo it. If it is not under tension it can shake loose. You can use it for just about everything from mooring the boat to tying a line to a bucket.

▲ Three fender knots: clove hitch, slipped clove hitch, round turn and two half hitches.

▲ Two rolling hitches: one for a rough surface, one for a smooth surface – a cow hitch and a rustler's hitch.

## TYING A BOWLINE

If you can remember a story about a rabbit, a hole and a tree you are in business, and the key to the knot is making the 'hole'.

▲ Draw a '6', the 'hole', in the end of the line.

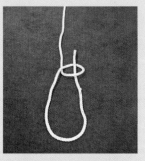

▲ Now take the working end of the line (the running end), or 'rabbit', up through the hole…

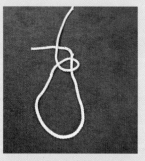

▲ and around the standing part of the rope, the 'tree'.

▲ Then back down the hole and pull tight on the three ends and you have a bowline.

## Clove hitch

Used for tying on fenders. I tie my fenders on with a slipped clove hitch. These undo with one tug on the slipped end and are very easy to adjust quickly. Ideal if you have to adjust the height of your fenders in a hurry. And I have never lost a fender tied on with a slipped clove hitch.

▲ Clove hitch.

▲ Slipped clove hitch.

## A CLOVE HITCH TO GO OVER A BOLLARD OR PALM HEAD

▲ Make two loops in the rope by taking the rope and twisting it clockwise for the first loop.

▲ And then twisting clockwise again make the second loop.

▲ Now take the right loop over the left loop.

▲ And drop this over the post and tighten.

## Round turn and two half hitches

A knot you can use for mooring. It will undo under tension. It is also useful for tying on fenders. If you tie them to the base of the stanchion, the weight of the fender hanging down tightens the running end of the knot and holds it secure. This is handy in marinas where there is a good deal of movement.

## Cow hitch

This is a very pretty knot, but that's about it. It can slip. I use it for hanging up wet ropes when I want things to look pretty.

▲ A round turn and two half hitches used to tie a fender to a stanchion.

▲ Cow hitch.

## Rolling hitch

This is a knot that binds. It does not have an obvious role to play on a motorboat, but you never know. A friend of mine wanted to tie a line to pull an electric cable with a very shiny coating through a long underground conduit the other day and I suggested he use a rolling hitch and it worked. The main thing I use this for is tying a snubber to the anchor chain once I have anchored. Tie a line to the chain with a rolling hitch and make this fast to a cleat on board and then pay out enough chain until the chain goes slack. Now the strain is being taken by the line and not your expensive windlass.

There are two ways to tie a rolling hitch. To get one rope to grip another you would tie it the traditional way where you cross the running end over the standing part as you make your turns. To tie a rope to a smooth surface you could make your turns on one side of the standing part before crossing over to finish the knot off.

▲ Left, a traditional rolling hitch, and right, a variation. Both work well. I find the variant works better on a smooth surface than the traditional.

## Slip knot

When might you need a slip knot? Say the boathook has gone in. The helm has got you back alongside and you cannot quite reach it, but you could slide the end of a rope over it. So you make a slip knot, snare the boathook with this, pull tight and retrieve it.

Scan the QR code to watch a video of these knots: bowline, clove hitch, round turn and two half hitches, cow hitch and rolling hitch.

▲ Take the running end of a piece of rope and make a bight by crossing it over the standing part.

▲ Take a bight of the standing part through this first bight.

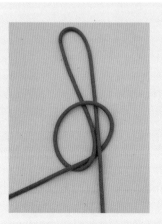

▲ Tighten the running end...

▲ and you have one slip knot.

I have also included a couple of knots that come from the climbers. If you have ever tried to attach something to anything vertical and smooth (say you want to hang something up, a lamp maybe for a little ambient light), you will have found it very difficult to get a knot to grip. Here are two knots that will bind on to that pole or post.

## Prusik knot
(pronounced Prussik)

Tie the ends of a piece of line together to make a loop. Now take one end of the loop round the post and bring the other end of the loop through the first loop, as you would for a 'strap hitch knot'. Do this again three more times. Make sure you even out the line so each part can grip on the rail. Pull tight and apply load. A Prusik knot will hold in both directions.

▶ Prusik knot.

## Klemheist

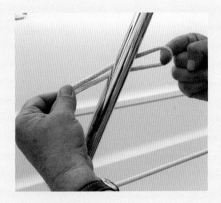

▲ Klemheist knot: the start.

▲ Six turns and then take the end through the bight.

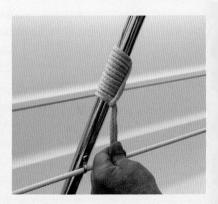

▲ Klemheist knot.

This is another knot that binds. It is simpler to tie than the Prusik knot. Again, join the line to make a continuous loop.

Take a bight of the loop behind the pole. Wrap the rest of the looped line round the pole a number of times (three to five). Take the remainder, the end of the line, and feed it through the bight at the top. Then apply the load. If you make sure that each part of the line is able to grip on the pole then it will lock solid when you apply the load.

▲ A lamp suspended from a pole with a Klemheist knot.

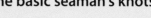

Now the best knot in the whole world:

## Rustler's hitch or highwayman's hitch

When you need a line, or something on the end of a line like a fender, in a hurry and yet you want it to be secure until you need it, this is the knot to use. The beauty is that, unlike other knots, the line in the rustler's hitch never actually goes around what you are attaching it to and that is why it will undo instantly. It doesn't look much, but it is a winner. I use it all the time.

I tell people that if you are going to rob a bank and if your chosen mode of transport for the day is to be a horse, that you will want the horse to be tied up securely to a rail outside the bank while you are about your business and yet when you have extracted the cash you will come flying out of the bank and want the horse to be free with one flick of your wrist. You cannot afford the time to undo a clove hitch or a round turn and two half hitches – you need the rustler's hitch. Is it a strong knot? Well, I have had fenders attached to a back rail, bouncing all over the shop as I have pounded into a heavy sea, and they didn't come off.

## TYING A RUSTLER'S HITCH

▲ Running end.

▲ Standing end.

▲ Take a bight of line under the rail.

▲ Reach through this bight.

▲ Then pick up the standing end.

▲ Pull this through the bight and tighten on the running end.

▲ Fingers through the bight you just made.

▲ Pick up the running end.

▲ Pull this through the bight and tighten on the standing end.

◀ Now the 'horse' will not get away and yet when you need the line all you have to do is yank on the running end and voilà!

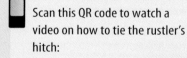 Scan this QR code to watch a video on how to tie the rustler's hitch:

## Tugboat bowline

Now here is something of a trick knot, a party piece if you like. If I want to tie a loop in the end of a line it will take me about seven seconds to create a bowline. I can tie a **tugboat bowline** in just over two seconds.

When everyone around has shown off their one-handed bowlines, you can really impress them with the tugboat bowline.

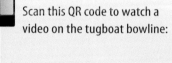

Scan this QR code to watch a video on the tugboat bowline:

## TYING A TUGBOAT BOWLINE

▲ The start.

▲ Flick the running end in the right hand over the two standing parts in the left.

▲ Take the bight in your right hand…

▲ through the bight in your left hand.

▲ Pull on the standing end.

▲ Tugboat bowline.

## REEF KNOT/THIEF KNOT

There is not much call for the reef knot on a boat. But did you know there is a knot that is very like the reef knot? It is just slightly different and it is called the thief knot. The idea was that you would tie up your kit bag with a thief knot and if anyone had undone this and tampered with your belongings, they would be bound to retie the kit bag with a reef knot, believing that was how it was tied in the first place. And so the owner would know they had been visited by a thief. I did this on a recent flight to Corfu, when I tied the handles of my travel grip together like this. And my thief knot was intact at the end. Of course, I don't suppose you need to open a bag if you can X-ray it.

▲ Reef knot: both ends on the same side.

▲ Thief knot: ends on different sides.

# THE BOATHOOK

It seems rather obvious to introduce the boathook, but there are a few things worth mentioning. First, boathooks should be used only for 'hoiking' things out of the briny. They should not be used for collision avoidance or fending off. A decent wooden-shafted boathook with a metal head will punch a hole straight through the GRP of the average modern boat if it is used as a lance. Fortunately modern boathooks have plastic heads and bendable aluminium shafts, so they should self-destruct before they can penetrate the GRP. Always place a fender between you and the impending accident, rather than try to fend off with a boathook.

The second thing is that when you want to grab a line, a float or whatever, you need to hold the boathook with the hook towards you, reach beyond what you want to grab, draw it towards you and up, for success every time.

If you have the hook the other way and you come from underneath and outwards you'll not always grab the line (or whatever you are trying for) first time, and if you do and it does not give, you can easily bend the boathook.

## HOOKED WITH SUCCESS

▲ Hold the boathook with the hook towards you.

▲ Reach beyond what you want to grab.

▲ Draw towards you...

▲ and up.

You can also use the boathook for offering up a line to a cleat. A boathook is just an extension of your arms. Don't try to overreach with this as it is jolly hard to hold the boathook at arm's length and hope to have any control over it. If you want to get a line on to a cleat at a range of about four feet from you, you can use the boathook.

To prevent a line from falling off the end of a boathook or out of the crook, tape the end to the boathook with some insulating tape. Once the loop or line is on the cleat, pull the boathook back sharply to break the tape. For success, once round with the tape will do. If you tape the boathook too well to the loop or line you may not be able to break it free. But this doesn't really matter as you'll be attached to the shore and can free the boathook later. You could use cotton wrapped round a few times rather than tape. Using the boathook to offer up lines down to the shore from high top-sided boats or up to a palm head in a lock is especially handy.

# HOW TO HOOK A CLEAT WITH A LINE

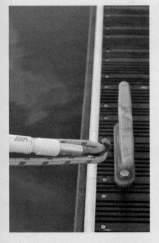

▲ Fit the line into the crook of the boathook and hold this tight.

▲ Then as you offer the line up to the cleat, allow a little slack.

▲ Thread the line on to the cleat…

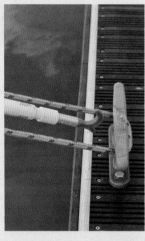

▲ and withdraw the boathook.

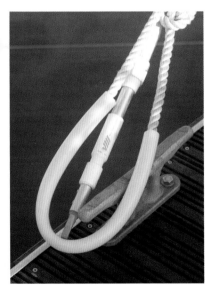

▲ You can offer up a bight/loop of line protected in a piece of plastic piping using the boathook.

▲ If you want to prevent the line from falling off the end of the boathook or out of the crook you can tape the line to it.

▲ You can do the same with line protected by plastic piping. The beauty is that it won't fall off.

# SLIPPING A BOWLINE LOOP OVER A CLEAT, BOLLARD OR PALM HEAD

▲ Bowline loop held in crook of boathook.

▲ Feeding the loop…

▲ over the…

▲ palm head.

▲ Done.

You also use the boathook as a means of communication. When picking up a mooring buoy, the crew can tell the helm where the buoy is by pointing the boathook obviously and directly at it. The helm also knows then which buoy the crew wants to aim for.

For extendable boathooks it is important to make sure they will extend quickly and that they have not seized. Getting alongside a buoy, grabbing the boathook and finding you cannot reach more than a few feet with it will be disappointing to say the least. A little silicone spray will do the trick to make sure the boathook will extend nicely. The boathook is then 'prepared'.

Of course, the minute you get the boathook out, you need to ready a slip knot, so that when it goes over the side and heads out to sea you can chase after it and retrieve it on board. Or, better still, you could tie a line from the boat to the boathook with rustler's hitches at

▼ Boathook attached to the boat by rustler's hitches on boathook and on boat.

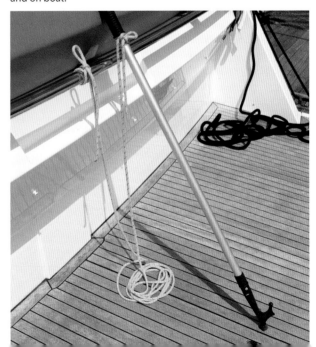

either end so the boathook would be attached to the boat if it went over and you could release it in an emergency.

And, finally, the boathook needs to be to hand.

▶ Boathook in the drink but not lost.

## SHARING A CLEAT

A standard Walcon cleat offers three places to which to attach a line: to either of the uprights or to the horizontal.

So if you want to add in a bow restrainer, add it into one side of the cleat to allow others to share the cleat.

### A shore line on a crowded cleat

If you are running a line ashore when rafted up and you see a cleat awash with other lines, tie a bowline into your line and feed it under everyone else's and over the top of the cleat. Now they can release your line to get theirs out and then put your line back when they have gone. In fact, each line can be removed independently. Mind you, if you are outboard of them in the raft and they are leaving, you will be involved one way or another in helping them.

This is a good reminder that if you're rafted up it is important to run lines ashore so that you take the strain of your boat on the shore cleats rather than on the boat you've just rafted alongside.

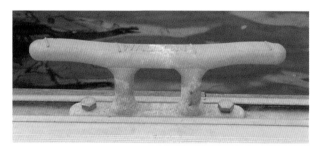

▲ Walcon cleat.

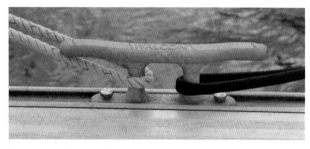

▲ How to share a Walcon cleat.

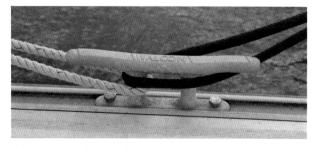

▲ How not to share a Walcon cleat.

▲ Sometimes you'll have to find a space for your shore line on a busy cleat like this.

▲ Tie a bowline into the end of your shore line and feed it under everyone else's and over the top of the cleat.

▲ If your shore line is attached like this, others in the raft can easily release it to get their lines out.

## KEEP A CLEAN HEAD

A smelly head makes the difference between a boat I want to sail on and a boat I want to get off.

### Why does the head smell?

There are tiny organisms living in sea or river water, and when you've finished pumping the head, either manually or electrically, there will be water left in the inlet pipe. There being no light or oxygen in the pipe, the organisms die and decompose. Anaerobic bacteria then take over and create unpleasant sulphurous gases. When you pump this through, you get the nasty smell.

These bacteria from both the water held in the inlet pipe and that held in the outlet pipe from what you pass through the head can, over time, penetrate and live inside the structure of the hoses, making your pipework smell.

### What can you do about it?

Putting disinfectant into the toilet bowl can help remove the problem from the toilet bowl and the outlet pipe, but doesn't reach the inlet pipe, and in any event will be flushed away the minute you pump the toilet.

You need the disinfectant to be introduced at the start of the system, down by the inlet seacock. But, of course, you can't get there very easily. There is a neat system from SeaSmart Marine (seasmartmarine.co.uk) where they stick a catheter down inside the inlet pipe and have a machine that doses the start of the run with disinfectant according to how much the toilet is used. This stops the nasty smell throughout the system. That is the only way I know that one can eliminate the odour. If you have problems, it makes sense to replace your pipework before getting a SeaSmart disinfectant system.

You may have a big boat with an on-board freshwater flush system, in which case you will not have the odour problem from anaerobic bacteria in the inlet pipe, as you will be using fresh drinking water which contains chlorine, fluoride compounds, salts, nitrate and pesticides, among other things. All of which will have killed off any organisms.

So water on the inlet side will be fresh. Smell can then be controlled by adding disinfectant to the toilet bowl. Denture cleaning tablets are good for this.

One way to establish if your pipework has been penetrated is to soak a towel in hot water and then wrap it around the pipe. If after the towel has cooled a nasty smell has been transferred to the towel, the pipe needs to be changed.

## Camping out on board

If space is at a premium, borrow from the caravan and camping set:

- Foldaway washing-up bowls
- Foldaway kettles
- Foldaway pots.

You don't have to have it in pink!

## Zip care

A little Vaseline on zips makes them run smoothly.

I operate a 'dry bowl' system aboard my boat and do not have any problem with odour. It may be that I use the boat so frequently that anaerobic bacteria don't have time to build up in the inlet pipe.

Another point is that I add nothing to my manual toilet, ever. The minute you add a little something, you make a rod for your own back because that toilet will need that little fix on a regular basis. If the pump action becomes a little stiff it is much better to take the pump section apart and apply a little silicone grease.

If you have sworn by a little something down the loo and have decided to move over to nothing you will find that the pump and system will squeak a bit at first in protest, but very shortly will settle down and function wonderfully sans olive oil, silicone, WD-40 or whatever patent additive you used to give it.

**Back spring (aft spring, stern spring)** Stops the stern moving backwards

**Bight** A U-shaped curve in a rope

**Head spring (forward spring, bow spring)** Stops the bow moving forward

**Loop** A fold or doubling of the rope through which another rope can be passed to form a knot or hitch

**Make fast** Tie off, secure

**Running end (aka working end)** The active end of the knot involved in making the knot

**Standing end** The end of the rope not involved in making the knot – the end attached to the fender, for example

**Standing part** The section between the knot and the standing end

**Warp** (noun) A rope used for manhandling a vessel, or for securing a vessel alongside a quay or jetty, for mooring

**Warp** (verb) To move the boat around using warps/rope

**Working end** The active end of the rope involved in making the knot

**Working part** The section between the knot and the working end

# 3 ENGINES

There are two things that are stressful about motorboating: parking (or mooring) and breaking down.

## DEALING WITH BREAKDOWNS

You can keep 'breaking down' to a minimum by being prepared, by understanding what is going on with an engine and by staying on top of servicing. By that I mean not just by having a mechanic service the engine(s) regularly, but by knowing what's going on, what's involved. It's a good idea to know how to change an air filter, an oil filter and a water/fuel separator and that the engine cooling system is working.

Breaking down is invariably indicated by a warning sound, an alarm.

## ALARMS

What makes alarms sound? We will have a look at all the occasions when an alarm goes off. The alarms for the various issues are all different and so it is worth

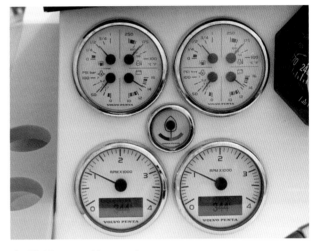

▲ All OK – everything matches.

checking out what each alarm sounds like. An alarm doesn't necessarily tell you what the problem is, simply that something is not quite right. You can ignore it, in which case things will stop working very shortly, or you can see what the problem is and probably do something about it. What might you be looking for?

### Oil pressure

This means no oil, or low oil pressure. No oil going round the crankshaft means that very shortly the engine will seize, so you need to stop the engine quickly. If you are in a narrow channel or precautionary area, keep going until you are out of it and then turn the engine off and anchor. You have about two to three minutes with no oil going round the engine before it will seize, enough to get out of harm's way but no more.

## TOP FIVE CAUSES OF BREAKDOWNS – OR WHY WON'T THE ENGINE START?

**1. Trying to start the engine while it's in gear**. Most engines will not start if the gear is engaged. Turn the key and you get nothing. You may get a buzzer or an alarm, but the engine won't turn over and you automatically assume there is something wrong with the electrics, perhaps a flat battery? Put the gear lever into neutral and the engine will start. This is a classic. You are on the flybridge, the engine won't start. Why? Because somehow the Morse control for the saloon helm is in gear. Some boats avoid this issue by having 'active control' where you press a button and make whichever controls you are at the active set. This overrides the other helm station. You still won't be able to start the engine at the active control if you have the Morse control in gear though.

**2. The quick-release fitting of the kill cord** (which all dinghy outboards, RIBs and many speedboats and sportsboats have) **has come out**. You wear the red lanyard round your wrist or leg, then stand up or reach over for something and it comes out. The engine stops. So you turn the key to start the engine. The engine will turn over but not start. Now you start to think there is some issue with the fuel, have you run out? Hopefully you will spot that the quick-release fitting has been pulled out and put it back. It is likely that the engine was in gear when you pulled the kill cord out and when you try to start the engine you'll get the buzzer or alarm and nothing. The engine won't turn over, because it is in gear. Back to No 1: put the lever into neutral, and the engine will start.

**3. Overheating**. A blockage in the cooling system? A heat exchanger issue? Has the fresh water leaked from the system? The engine has been automatically shut down. Find the source of the problem, fix, override the shutdown and restart the engine.

**4. One of the engine start battery terminals has come off**. Put it back on, securely.

**5. Running out of fuel**.
'But the fuel gauge says we still have half a tank left!'
'The fuel gauge is wrong, sir.'
What can I say?

Of course, all the time you run the engine with no oil pressure you will be damaging the bearings and you will probably create some long-term damage.

## Overheating

Raw-water blockage. It is worth noting that with many shaft drives the exhaust is led out of the boat at or slightly above the waterline, so you can see the water coming out of the exhaust, so you know that the raw water is getting through the system and is being pumped round. Some designers of shaft drive boats lead the exhaust underwater to reduce the sound and then, of course, you cannot see water coming out of the exhaust. Stern drives always have the exhaust outlet underwater.

In the engine room you can see the raw-water strainer, although it's hard to see what is happening in there because when running it should be full of water

**TOP TIP**

### Avoiding snapped cables

One problem for which there is no warning is a broken throttle cable or gear linkage from the Morse control. This will result either in no revs beyond tick over for a throttle cable, or in your not being able to engage ahead or astern for a gear linkage break. Replacing these cables every five years is a good way to reduce the risk of a snap. If you notice any stiffness about the throttle or the gear, check the cables and replace if necessary.

and you don't really see anything. If the strainer is not quite full of water and there are bubbles and you can see the water running through the strainer, then something is not quite right and you have a blockage or the impeller in the pump is not pulling the water through. So you need to check this.

Simon of *Evelyn*, which is moored on the river, has marked on the side of the hull exactly where the raw-water intakes are, so he can get a long-handled brush to them either from on board or from the shore, in case he has picked up debris or a plastic bag.

I know this because I was on *Evelyn* when an alarm went off. We were on the Thames at the time. You don't know what the alarm means so you scan the instrument panel. Any needle (on a twin-engined boat) that is not matching its partner is likely to be where the problem lies. We could see that the port engine was much hotter than the starboard engine. So, while running on the starboard engine throughout to maintain way, we were able to shut the port engine down, check it and then start it up and run it, and we clearly saw that the strainer was half full of water. A blockage, then, and as there was plenty of suction coming from the impeller, the blockage had to be at the raw-water inlet.

We moored. Simon got out a brush and had a poke around and cleared what debris we had collected. With the engine restarted, the strainer filled perfectly and all was fixed. It was after that on a lift out that Simon decided to mark the spots of the raw-water intakes. That's a nice example of preparation.

Of course, any alarm going off on a nice peaceful potter along a river alarms not just those on the boat but everyone within about a one-mile radius. So everyone knows that you have a problem. There is nothing discreet about an alarm. Mind you, I suppose that's the point.

It is also very alarming when an alarm goes off. Your first instinct is to panic! The alarm is so loud. But this is one case where the adage 'Do nothing, first' applies. The alarm goes, look at the instrument panel. Don't immediately shut anything down because you don't know what to shut down, and with engines shut down, you won't see anything. Look at the panel. Is anything out of the ordinary? Let's investigate that. If you're flying along at full chat and an alarm goes off then throttle back, but do not shut down the engines.

▲ Simon's brush.

▲ Handle noting the need to raise the leg 12° and note marking when the brush is by the inlet. That's attention to detail.

▶ It's a long brush.

▲ Position marked on hull.

▲ Simon with brush in place – note the mark on the hull.

## Ping-pong trick

To check if the raw water is flowing nicely, put a ping-pong ball into the strainer. This will float at the top and you will see it bobbing about to let you know that the flow is going well.

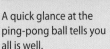

A quick glance at the ping-pong ball tells you all is well.

No ping-pong ball? It's hard to tell if the strainer is full or not.

## Hands-on check

Want to check if raw water is flowing nicely? With the engine running, put your hand on the impeller faceplate. If it is cool, all is well. If it is hot, you have a problem. This tip is useful when you have a stern-drive engine where you cannot see the raw water coming out of the exhaust as it is underwater.

## Not charging

The alternator is not charging batteries, perhaps because the alternator belt is broken or slipping.

The alternator belt also runs the fresh-water pump in a heat exchanger-cooled engine, so if the alternator belt is broken or slipping the fresh-water pump will not be running and the engine will start to overheat.

Generally the raw-water pump runs directly off the engine, but in some engines it can run off the alternator belt and, again, if there was a problem with the belt this would not be running and the engine would be overheating. Incidentally, on those engines where the raw-water pump does run off an alternator belt, the impeller faceplate normally faces backwards, so it is harder to reach if you're checking the temperature or if you're changing an impeller.

## Raw-water flow

There is no sea water or raw water flowing round the system: overheating is about to happen.

## Battery charging light

This tells you that the battery is no longer being charged by the alternator. This may be because there is a problem with the drive belt, perhaps it is broken, perhaps it is slipping. It is not driving the alternator. If this is the case it will not be driving the raw-water pump impeller either and overheating may result. If there is nothing wrong with the drive belt and the raw-water system is flowing fine, then there is another issue, which will be associated with the alternator and which needs to be checked by a mechanic.

## Exhaust

An exhaust alarm is rare and is usually an after-market fit, so don't assume that you have one. It is telling you that the exhaust is too hot. This is because there is no raw water coming through. You have a problem with the raw-water intake, the strainer, the impeller. This exhaust alarm pre-empts the engine overheating. It is an indicator that you are about to have a problem.

## Fire safety system

The fire safety alarm could mean two things:

**1 You have a fire in the engine room, or an engine has overheated** to the point that it has triggered the fire safety system. The system will deploy the fire

## Outboard storage

How to carry an outboard? Never lift the prop end higher than the head because standing water in the waterways around the prop will run down the leg and corrode the bottom crank bearing. If the engine is a four-stroke make sure you lay it down on its correct side. One way will be fine, the other will allow oil to leak out. Check the manual.

extinguishers, and if you have a fire safety system that cuts out the engines, these will be stopped. Not all fire safety systems cut the engines though. If your system does, you will have a manual override switch.

To check if you have a fire, feel the engine room cover or door. If hot, you may have a fire. Do not open any doors or covers to the engine, as this will introduce oxygen and accelerate the flames.

**Call the Coastguard or 999.**

**2** **Your fire extinguishers are low on pressure** and this is sensed by the fire safety system in the engine room. Generally this happens because the fire extinguishers have not been serviced. You should have all fire extinguishers serviced annually. The service includes checking the weight to make sure that there is the correct amount of gas in the cylinder, checking for corrosion, and a pressure gauge test. You can check the weight of the cylinders and see if there is any corrosion, but you can't do the pressure gauge test – that has to be done at a service centre.

If you have the fire extinguishers serviced annually then the extinguisher can go on more or less for ever. If you choose the alternative route – that is, to save on the servicing costs – then you will find that the extinguishers have a use-by date, which means that without any servicing the extinguisher will be good up to that date. Afterwards it may lose pressure, and that may be why the fire safety system is sounding an alarm.

If the engine covers are cool, hit the override switch, start the engines and make for shallow water, anchor or moor up and see what the problem was.

## Water in fuel

The sensor has detected that water is in the fuel. You can drain the water out of the water separator filter.

If this doesn't fix the problem and the alarm continues, it may be that there is a lot of water in the fuel tank, and this is a more serious issue that will require the tank(s) to be drained and the source of the water ingress to be established and repaired.

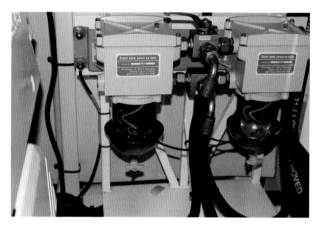

▲ Fuel filters and water/fuel separators.

## Bilge pumps

There is water in the bilges and this has risen above the safe level, which is why the alarms have sounded. Investigate. Most boats will have a panel that shows whereabouts on the vessel the activated bilge alarm is located. A light will indicate this.

## Fit the spare

That way you know how to fit the spare when you need to, and you know that the new one works. You also know that the original worked, so you have a spare that works.

## Smoke

You can learn quite a bit from smoke, and not all smoke is an indication of impending doom.

## White smoke

White smoke is water vapour. So somewhere along the line water has been heated up so that it becomes vapour. This could be for a number of reasons. Perhaps there is too little raw water passing through the hot exhaust. If the volume of water passing through is at the standard operating level then there will be little or no water vapour or white smoke. So too little water arriving at the exhaust can mean that there is a raw-water blockage at the raw-water inlet, a blockage at the strainer or an impeller malfunctioning, which might be caused by broken vanes on the impeller or by the belt slipping.

If you've checked these and found that all are working fine and that there is actually a good level of raw water flowing through, there must be another reason for the water vapour. The engine might be burning water internally as a result of a blown head gasket, cracked exhaust manifold, cracked cylinder liner or cracked cylinder head.

One way of establishing this on a heat exchanger-cooled engine is to check the level of the fresh water. There will be excess pressure within the header tank, so you need to be careful when removing the header tank cap. Put a towel over the cap and turn it slowly while applying downward pressure to counteract the excess pressure in the system and gradually allow the pressure to release. Then, rather than putting a finger down into the header tank, dip it with something else to check the level of the water – it will be hot! Of course, if the engine was overheating you'd expect an alarm to go off. There is no way of telling if a direct-cooled engine has blown a head gasket or has a cracked cylinder other than that the engine will probably be misfiring.

## Black smoke

Black smoke is diesel in the exhaust, due to inefficient burning of diesel by the engine. This could be as a result of overloading the engine. Reasons for this are possibly a very dirty hull, dragging a lot of weed through the water or a barnacle-encrusted propeller. Once the smoke has cleared you can see black soot on the water. This is often mistaken for oil on the water, when actually it is soot. Oil on the water will give you a rainbow effect. The way to resolve a black smoke issue is to stop overloading the engine by making sure the hull is clean and that the propeller is clear of deposits.

## Blue smoke

Blue smoke means oil in the exhaust gas mix. Most diesel engines give off a little blue smoke when they first start. This burns off as they warm up and the engine comes under load. If you have blue smoke while going along it indicates that you have a lot of engine wear – an old engine – and it is likely to get worse. It can also be a sign that a piston ring is on its way out and that will damage the engine.

## Understanding engine cooling

Most marinised engines are cooled indirectly with a closed cooling system of fresh water, which in turn is cooled by raw water via a heat exchanger. The raw water is sucked in through the inlet because of the raw-water pump that is driven by the drive belt from the engine, which also drives the alternator. The closed fresh-water system will have a header/expansion tank. Check the level of this regularly and top up where necessary. Then as long as raw water is being pumped through the system and exiting the exhaust, the fresh-water system should keep the engine at the required operating temperature.

Some engines just have a raw-water cooling system. These tend to be petrol engines and they were designed to be used on lakes with fresh water. When they are used in sea water they corrode quickly and the engine components have a short service life, comparable to the service life of heat exchangers on indirect cooling systems.

When buying a boat it is important to check out the cooling system for the engine(s) in case you are looking at a direct raw-water cooling system and you intend to use the boat in a different environment from that for which the cooling system was intended.

# FUEL CONSUMPTION AND ECONOMY

It is a fact that the faster you go the more fuel you will use and the more it will cost. Fuel economy, though, does not follow a straight line in relation to speed, because there are occasions when going a bit faster will actually improve economy – economy being the cost to travel a certain distance.

All boats will be at their most economical when in displacement mode, although boats that are designed for planing will not necessarily be as economical in displacement mode as those designed for displacement mode only.

## Displacement hull

A displacement hull is designed to drive through the water and will have a maximum speed attainable which is directly related to the length along the waterline.

This is called the hull speed and it can be calculated for any given boat. It is 1.34 x the √ LWL (length along the waterline) in feet. This formula, known as the Speed to Length Ratio (SLR), refers to the distance between the bow and stern wave crests – one wavelength.

▲ Displacement hull.

### Speed to Length Ratio i

Imperial: 1.34 x √ LWL in feet = speed in knots

Metric: 2.45 x √ LWL in metres = speed in knots

As a boat goes faster than its hull speed so it starts to climb the bow wave. At the same time the stern sinks down into the trough in the water caused by the boat's forward movement.

▲ As this boat climbs the bow wave, the stern is sinking into the trough. The boat is going faster than its hull speed.

## Semi-displacement hull

A semi-displacement hull is designed to lift out of the water and on top of the bow wave with added 'lift' aft to counter the stern sinking. It will be able to travel faster than a displacement-hulled boat.

▲ Semi-displacement hull: the boat is climbing the bow wave ahead and is straddling two waves.

# Planing

A planing hull is designed to climb out of the water and to 'hydro-plane', hence 'planing'. It takes a lot more power to climb over the bow wave and get the boat out of the water than it does to maintain the boat on the plane. On the plane there is less wetted area and less resistance.

Displacement and semi-displacement boats will have smaller engines than a planing boat because it takes an enormous amount of power to get the planing boat over the bow wave and up on to the plane.

A planing boat will quickly climb the bow wave and get up on the plane. Generally they start to plane at around the top end of the semi-displacement hull speeds, roughly 18 knots, revs about 2500. In terms of efficiency, though, it is important to increase revs so the boat is well

on the plane, because if you stay at the speed it requires to get up on to the plane you will have to adjust the trim tabs to raise the stern and so will increase drag and increase fuel consumption. Planing at between 3000 and 3500 is generally the most economical.

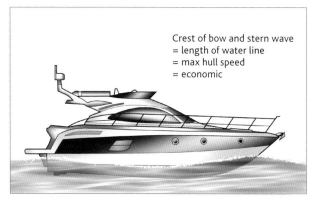

Crest of bow and stern wave
= length of water line
= max hull speed
= economic

▲ Displacement.

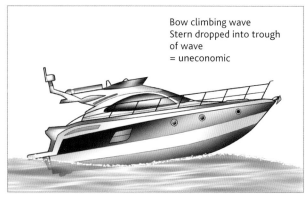

Bow climbing wave
Stern dropped into trough of wave
= uneconomic

▲ Semi-displacement.

▲ Planing boat.

## e An example of hull speed

A boat with an overall length (LOA) of 40ft and a length along the waterline (LWL) of 35ft will have a maximum displacement hull speed of:

$\sqrt{35ft} = 5.92 \times 1.34 = 8$ knots.

A semi-displacement hull will improve the SLR to between 3 and 3.5 the $\sqrt{}$ of the LWL in feet, so our 40ft LOA/35ft LWL boat will be able to go at between 18 and 21 knots.

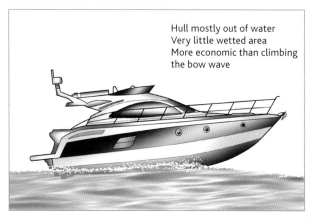

Hull mostly out of water
Very little wetted area
More economic than climbing the bow wave

▲ Planing.

Going flat out increases fuel consumption enormously. It is generally considered that a boat will use twice as much fuel flat out on the plane as it will when just on the plane at 2500 revs, but as stated above, at the 2500 revs level this is not particularly fuel efficient. Everyone should know the fuel efficiency of their boat. Monitoring the average is one way you can keep track of fuel in the tanks, despite what the fuel gauge may be telling you. With a planing boat it's also worth checking what fuel consumption or efficiency you get in the three states (displacement, cruising on the plane and flat out on the plane).

You can improve efficiency by using the tide, of course. Imagine your boat uses 200 litres when going at 30 knots. If you decided to go against a tidal race that was running at 5 knots, at the end of an hour of travelling at 30 knots you would have covered only 25 miles over the ground. You would still have 5 miles to go. And so you would use 35 miles' worth of diesel to go 30 miles, the tide knocking you back by 5 miles. So you would use 233 litres. At 90p a litre it would cost you an extra £30. But if you went with the tide you would use only 25 miles' worth of diesel to go the 30 miles, as the tide would push you at 5 knots. So you would use 167 litres. A saving of £30. The difference between your saving going with the tide and the extra going against is £60. Worth considering.

### Fuel consumption

| Mode | Type of hull design | | |
|---|---|---|---|
| | Displacement | Semi-displacement | Planing |
| Hull speed | 1 | 1 | 1 |
| Planing, cruising speed | | 2 | |
| Climbing the bow wave – semi-displacement | 2 | 2 | 3 |
| Planing flat out | | 4 | |

And here are the stats for a Bavaria 32 planing boat that support this:

### Example: Bavaria 32

| Displacement | 7 knots | 9.3 litre/hour | 0.75 nautical miles/litre |
|---|---|---|---|
| Semi-displacement | 9.4 knots | 24.3 l/h | 0.39 nm/l |
| Planing | 22.2 knots | 38.1 l/h | 0.58 nm/l |
| Flat out | 32.8 knots | 87.5 l/h | 0.37 nm/l |

### The cost of going against the tide for varying rates of tide (diesel at 90p per litre)

| Litres per hour | £@ 90p/l | 1 knot | 2 knots | 3 knots | 4 knots | 5 knots |
|---|---|---|---|---|---|---|
| 45 | 40.50 | 42 | 43 | 45 | 47 | 49 |
| 90 | 81.00 | 84 | 87 | 90 | 93 | 97 |
| 135 | 121.50 | 126 | 130 | 133 | 140 | 146 |
| 180 | 162.00 | 168 | 173 | 180 | 187 | 194 |
| 275 | 247.50 | 256 | 265 | 275 | 286 | 297 |
| 360 | 324.00 | 335 | 347 | 360 | 374 | 389 |

### The saving by going with the tide

| Litres per hour | £@ 90p/l | 1 knot | 2 knots | 3 knots | 4 knots | 5 knots |
|---|---|---|---|---|---|---|
| 45 | 40.50 | 39 | 38 | 37 | 36 | 35 |
| 90 | 81.00 | 78 | 76 | 74 | 71 | 69 |
| 135 | 121.50 | 118 | 114 | 110 | 107 | 104 |
| 180 | 162.00 | 157 | 152 | 147 | 143 | 139 |
| 275 | 247.50 | 240 | 232 | 225 | 218 | 212 |
| 360 | 324.00 | 313 | 304 | 295 | 286 | 278 |

And for a boat that does 500 litres an hour at 30 knots, going against the 5-knot tide would cost an additional £75 and going with it would save £75. The difference is a whopping £150.

The fuel-consumption table shows the costs of going against different strengths of tide. And it goes without saying that keeping the hull clean is a key part of getting the best fuel economy.

### Just a tick

Did you realise that in tickover your boat really uses very little fuel? Even the mighty Princess 23M *Lucky Ash* at 76 foot uses only 3 litres/hour per engine in tickover. Put it into gear in tickover and this rises to 9 litres/hour. At 90p a litre x 18, that is just £16.20 an hour. And it goes through the water at 6.7 knots on tickover. You've only got to add in a couple of knots of favourable tide to have a very reasonable speed over ground. Flat out on the plane, of course, doing 33 knots it will use 500 litres/hour, which is an eye-watering £450. See what your tickover fuel consumption is. If you don't need to go flat out all the time, you could save some money.

# 4 CONTROLLING THE BOAT

Looking at a boat sitting in the water, you have little idea what is under the keel in terms of propulsion, and there are a number of options, from a single propeller on a shaft with a rudder to 360° rotatable pods with counter-rotating prop drives. And they all behave slightly differently.

## TYPES OF PROPULSION

### Shaft drive

The engine is inboard, the drive is inboard and the shaft, prop and rudder are outboard.

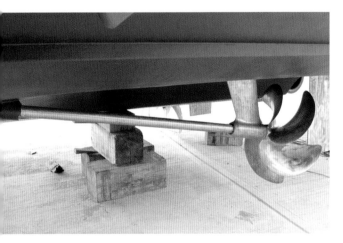

▲ Shaft drive.

### Stern drive

The engine is inboard, but the drive is outboard and with the propeller acts as a rudder to steer the boat.

▲ Twin- (top) and single-engined outdrives.

## Outboard

The engine, drive, prop etc. are outside the boat. You steer by turning the entire engine.

▶ Outboard.

## Pod drives

The engines are inboard, and pods under the hull that turn through 360° allow the boat to be manoeuvred in any direction.

▶ Volvo Penta IPS pod with twin counter-rotating propellers.

## Jet thrust

The engines are inboard, and nozzles outboard send jets of water to propel the boat. Steering is by turning the nozzles or angling the jets.

A note about jet thrust boats: they are fast, highly manoeuvrable, possibly a little unresponsive at low speeds and awkward to handle about the dock, and therefore tend to require thrusters.

▶ Hamilton jet thrust propulsion.

## Thrusters

You can also add in electric bow thrusters and stern thrusters. These are available as the standard through-hull propeller type or as jet thrusters. The advantages of jet thrusters over propeller thrusters are that they are much quieter (pretty much silent), there is no propeller to foul, they can be fitted more or less anywhere on the boat and can therefore be set at the extremities for greater effect, and they are easy to install.

▲ Bow thruster.

▲ Stern thruster.

# WHAT CAN YOU EXPECT?

## Single engine

It will have a slight kick in ahead in one direction or the other, depending on whether it has a right-handed or left-handed prop. Right-handed props will kick to starboard in ahead and left-handed props will kick to port.

It will have a more pronounced kick when going astern. Right-handed props kick to port astern and left-handed props kick to starboard.

To find out which way a single-engined boat will kick when going astern, make sure it is tied securely to the dock and then put it into astern. Look down each side: one side will have calm water, the other will have turbulent water. The boat will kick in the direction of the calm water. If you can't see much difference between the two sides, increase the revs, or get the helm to give a quick burst of revs astern, and whichever side turbulence appears, the boat will kick towards the other side. If you need to increase the revs or give a quick burst to see the turbulence, it means the boat will not have much of a kick when going astern.

You will use these kicks to your advantage. Mooring port-to with a right-handed prop? Then a burst of astern will walk the boat in towards the dock. The same applies for a left-handed prop and mooring starboard-to. If you can arrange your berth so that whether you enter bows first or stern first and into the tide or stream, by clicking the engine into astern (bows in) or ahead (stern in) you will tuck the boat alongside.

You can also turn the boat in a tight circle. It will have a favoured turn. If the boat kicks to port in astern this will be a turn to starboard and if it kicks to starboard in astern this will be to port.

## Twin engines

All twin-engined boats will be set so that the outer drive or shaft when in astern will kick the stern into the dock. The inner drive will kick the boat off the dock in astern.

# HOW TO MAKE YOUR BOAT GO SIDEWAYS

## Pod drives

Well, this is easy, you just point the joystick in the direction you want to go. Sideways? Point it sideways. Do note that although the IPS does send you sideways it can also introduce a little movement ahead or astern. Check this on your boat and then you will be able to allow for it. There is one drawback to the IPS, and that is that the pods are placed at the stern, and on the boats

▲ *Evelyn*, port ahead, starboard astern, thrusting the bow to port, is going sideways to port. See the wash of the thruster on the starboard bow.

I have been on there was no bow thruster. I would want a bow thruster because there are occasions when a strong wind will blow the bow off and the IPS does not have the power (operating from the stern) to hold the bow up to the wind.

## 2 x shafts and 1 x bow thruster

Centre the rudders. Oppose the engines and thrust the bow in the direction of the engine that is in ahead. So port ahead, starboard astern, thrust the bow to port and you will go sideways to port. Again, there can be some movement ahead or astern with this and this is something you need to check and adjust for by increasing the revs slightly on one engine to counter the movement. Check this out in a bit of space.

## 2 x stern drives and 1 x bow thruster

As for 2 x shafts, although here you have the opportunity to angle the drives to help with the sideways movement. Experiment until you can go sideways with no movement ahead or astern.

## 1 x shaft drive and 1 x bow thruster

Here, even though you are not able to oppose the engines, you can still make a pretty good stab at going sideways. Want to go to port? Helm hard astarboard, add in the thruster taking the bow to port and then click the engine into ahead. The stern will be pushed to port by the drive from the prop off the rudder at the same time as you are thrusting the bow to port and the boat will go to port. Balance the two forces – if the engine is turning the bow to starboard too much (because the wash off the rudder is pushing the stern to port) and is overpowering the thruster, then put the engine into neutral for a moment, until the bow thruster catches up. You may introduce a small amount of movement ahead, but when we tried this on *Katcha*, a Broom 29, it worked well.

## 1 x stern drive and 1 x bow thruster

As above. Helm hard astarboard, thruster taking the bow to port, click the engine into ahead and you should move sideways. Again, movement ahead might be experienced. As with all exercises, give yourself plenty of space and experiment.

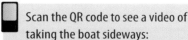 Scan the QR code to see a video of taking the boat sideways:

# BOATS STEER LIKE FORKLIFT TRUCKS AND DUMPER TRUCKS – FROM THE BACK

It is important to consider that, unlike a car, where, when you turn the wheel to the right the front wheels follow suit and take the car to the right, in a boat, when you turn the helm to the right, to starboard, it is not the bow that moves to the right but the stern that moves to the left, and this makes the bow move to the right.

If you are about to hit something on your port side, therefore, the last thing you need to do is turn to starboard because this will send your stern to port and straight into what you are trying to avoid. It is counter-intuitive, but to avoid something on port you need to turn to port to throw your stern away from it. You then need to stop and back out of the situation.

Boats pivot from a point about a third of the way from the bow when going ahead, and from a point about a third of the way from the stern when going astern.

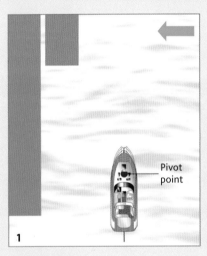

**1**

Pivot point

▲ Wind pushing us…

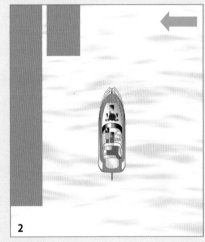

**2**

▲ towards…

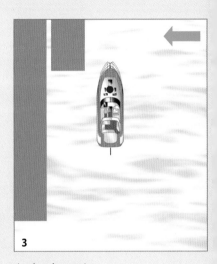

**3**

▲ the obstruction.

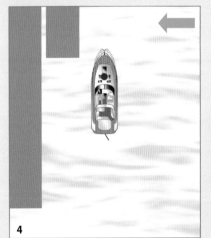

**4**

▲ Turn to starboards to avoid it?

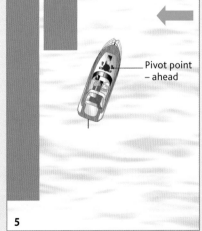

**5**

Pivot point – ahead

▲ Um…

**6**

▲ Perhaps not!

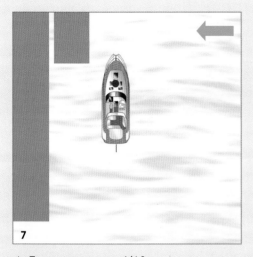

▲ Turn to port … to avoid it?

▲ Better. Now go astern to stop…

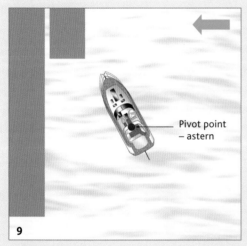

Pivot point – astern

▲ Back away…

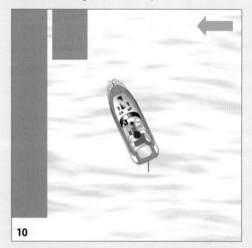

▲ And with room … port helm astern…

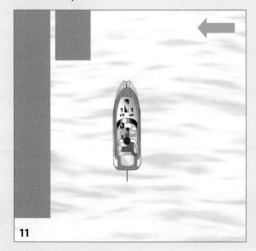

▲ to square up again…

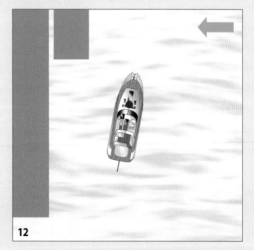

▲ And now ahead, countering the wind.

## Bow thrusting

A word about bow thrusting. Most people put the bow thruster on for a burst of about one second at a time. When going sideways you need a burst of about ten seconds. It seems like an eternity. It isn't. If you take the bow thruster out or the engine out at any point you will ruin the balance of the occasion and you will not go sideways. Make sure you have space, and be bold! Every time we failed to make a boat go sideways it was because the helm had taken the bow thruster out. Ten seconds is all you need to go sideways – count it out on your fingers – and imagine you had the thruster on for this time.

I spoke to Vetus about sensible use of a thruster. Ten seconds is fine. They said that if you held it in for **two and a half minutes** solidly you might want to allow it to cool down for an hour before using it again. Have you any idea how long two and a half minutes is? Well, it is unthinkable. So thrusting for 10 seconds, 15 seconds, 20 seconds in one constant burst will not burn out the thruster. Of course, if you do this for ten-second periods one after the other and add up to two and half minutes in the hour then you need to give it a rest for an hour before doing it again. Actually, the figure that Vetus gave me was well in excess of 2' 30", but I don't want anyone suffering heart failure and I think you might if I told you.

As with anything, you have to find the balance so that the boat moves sideways gracefully, with no fore and aft movement. But once mastered, this is a technique that can get you out of a very tight berth with ease, or into one, of course.

## Bow and stern thrusters

If you have bow and stern thrusters you will have read the above and wondered what on earth all the fuss was about, as you can go sideways any time you like.

# TURNING THE BOAT 180° IN ITS OWN LENGTH

It is very useful to be able to spin the boat round in its own length. And this is very easy to achieve with:

- Bow thruster and stern thruster: oppose them and the boat will spin round.

- Twin shaft drives: oppose the engines. To speed up the rate of the turn, increase the revs on one engine, either the one ahead or the one astern.

- Twin stern drives: centre the helm and oppose the engines. Again, increasing the revs on either one of the engines will speed up the rate of the turn.

- Single engine and bow thruster: bow thruster only.

- Single engine, no bow thruster: turn in the direction opposite that in which you kick when in astern. Kick to starboard astern? Then the crash turn is to port. Helm hard aport, burst of power ahead. This kicks water off the rudder and pushes the stern to starboard, which gets the bow moving to port. Keep the stern going to starboard by clicking the engine into astern and using the prop walk to walk the stern around. Then back into ahead and another burst. And into astern to keep the momentum going. Keep doing this until you get round. You may not make the turn entirely in your own length but it will be very nearly so.

I have not gone into the question of trim tab use here. Tabs are for balancing the horizontal aspect of the boat and how it sits in the water, bows up or bows down and are something you adjust to get the most balanced ride and the best fuel economy.

It is important to take your boat out into a bit of open space and play with it to see how it behaves. This is all part of your preparation. If you know what the boat does, you will know how to control it.

 Scan the QR code to watch a video of turning a single prop boat 180° in its own length:

## Twin-engined boat using one engine only

Twin-engined boat? With both engines on, practise driving under one engine only to see what happens. The boat will steer in the opposite direction to the side the engine is on. Port engine only will steer the boat to starboard, starboard engine only will steer the boat to port. Counter this with the rudders to steer a straight line.

Now do the same, but turn one engine off each time. Why? Because the hydraulics for the steering will be powered by one of the engines. Try turning off the starboard engine (the hydraulics are usually powered by this engine) and, with the port engine running, see what the steering is like. It will be very heavy without any assistance – indeed, it may actually not be possible to steer the boat. It's worth checking.

## A WOBBLE a day keeps disaster at bay

Daily engine checks:

**W** (Water): Fresh water, check the header tank.

**O** (Oil): Engine oil, check. Periodically check gearbox oil as well.

**B** (Belt): Alternator belt, looks OK? Tension OK? Half an inch of play.

**B** (Battery): Topped up, terminals look OK?

**L** (Leaks): Any nasty leaks under the engine?

**E** (Exhaust): Water coming out of the exhaust when the engine is running?

# 5 THE BERTH

Your berth in a marina is the one place that you will spend most time coming in and out of – set things up so that they are as easy as possible.

## FIXINGS TO THE SHORE

These vary from bollards, T cleats and hooped cleats to palm heads, rings, stakes you will drive into the river bank and posts. Some marinas still use rings. As they update they are all heading towards T cleats as the favoured option.

The techniques I describe are immediately useful where you are able to get a line around anything, T cleat, bollard, palm head, post etc. Where you have to thread a line through a ring, you have to help yourselves. This is where preparation and ingenuity come into play. Take a line with an eye splice in it, attach it to the ring, fix a perch to the dock to hold your line and grab this when you arrive at your berth and place it over a cleat on board. The helm can drive against this to hold the boat alongside, all managed from on board.

▲ T cleat.

Or you could just have a line attached to the ring on the ground, which you can grab with the boathook and place round the stern cleat to drive against. It's all about preparation.

Across the Channel in France they often have hooped cleats (*taquet d'amarrage cerclé*) for the residents in a marina, but there are generally also T cleats. There may be a hooped cleat or bar at the end of the finger, but if there is a T cleat by the shore then you can moor stern-to, lasso this and drive ahead against it.

Note: It is essential to make sure that anything you intend to lasso and then drive the boat against is up to the job. Do check this out beforehand, for both cleats on shore and cleats on board.

▲ Small T cleat.

▲ Hooped cleat.

▲ Bollard.

▲ Handrail of a ladder for climbing out of the river.

▲ Rings.

▲ Post.

▲ Palm head.

▲ A line ready on the post.

▲ Over the top for greater security.

## WHICH SIDE TO MOOR

Deciding which side to moor is important. With a gate from the cockpit to a bathing platform on the port side it will be more convenient to moor port-to. If it is on the other side then starboard-to will be most convenient. But if the flybridge helm position is on starboard, it will be more difficult to see when mooring port-to. If you are lucky you will have the gate on port and the flybridge helm on port. Of course, the saloon helm position is invariably on starboard – although this presents less difficulty when mooring port-to as you can see the stern side deck from the saloon, just about.

If the berth you have been allocated does not meet your needs, get yourself on the list for a change. Marina berths are moving all the time as people buy and sell boats and move into and out of the sport.

▲ Here's a perch on which this berth holder stores his lines.

▶ The large boat that lives here keeps the bow line ready to hand with this perch. One crew member grabs this and makes it fast to the bow while another crew member lassoes a stern cleat. The boat is secure.

▶▶ And now the boat is on the berth.

## NEIGHBOURS

When it comes to marinas and finger pontoons where you have a neighbour on the other side, who you share with is important. It is much better that motorboats share with motorboats and sailing boats with sailing boats. There are two striking differences between the two, one being that sailing boats are strongest just at the point that motorboats are weakest, amidships, and the other being the height difference. The gunwale of a 50ft yacht will be well below the gunwale of a 50ft motorboat and so the motorboater has to allow for this when setting fenders between them. Fenders will need to be not just to gunwale height but lower. It is much easier for a motorboat to moor next to another motorboat than next to a yacht.

## FENDERS

You could dispense with fenders altogether on the dockside by adding a fender dock. On the side by a neighbour, you will need fenders set at your gunwale height, or possibly lower than this if they are a yacht.

▲ Motorboats and yachts, being different shapes and heights, are not ideal neighbours in finger berths.

▼ Fender dock means there is no need for fenders at your home berth.

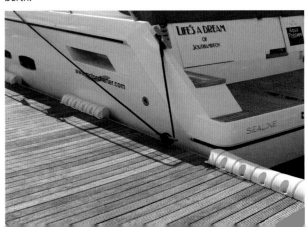

## Step ashore

Bathing platform too far from the dock to step on conveniently? Rather than try to haul the boat closer to the dock by hand if it is too far away to step on, hang on to a cleat on board and just put your foot on the stern line, apply a little weight and this will bring the boat into the dock. Now step aboard.

Too far to step across.

Better.

And step across.

# MOORING WARPS

Why not have preset lines? This is your home berth, you will always be in the same place in the berth. You will probably berth stern-to and if on occasion you do decide to go bows-to then you can forget the preset lines and use conventional mooring warps.

You could attach the lines to the cleats with a shackle and have an eye splice at the other end to go round the cleat on the boat. The line would be spliced to exactly the right length. This would work for the bow line, the head spring or forward spring (which stops the bows from moving forwards) and the back spring or aft spring (which stops the stern moving backwards). It

would be an idea to keep the stern line short and open ended and to operate this from the boat. So bow line and springs stay on the dock and the stern line stays on the boat. You'll use this as a 'spring' line to drive against when getting off the dock and when getting on (see Chapters 6 and 7).

# POSITIONING

Knowing when you are in the correct position within the berth once you have arrived is key. And this doesn't have to rely on guesswork or instruction from the crew in the cockpit who are shouting above the noise of the engines. Remember that if you are on the flybridge or the helm in the saloon, there are a couple of very large and noisy engines between you and the crew standing in the cockpit. Added to which, the crew has the noise of the props and the swirling water to contend with.

And here's a thought. Make sure that both crew and helm understand the measurement that's being given. When you are approaching the dock, one foot is a lot closer than one yard!

▼ Lines shackled to the cleats.

## How long should your bow line be?

It should not be long enough for one end to reach the propeller when the other end is attached to a bow cleat. Shorter than this and you are in business. Longer and you may have a problem if you allow it to fall in the drink and it makes its way to the stern.

Stern lines can generally be quite short. Of course, if you are mooring to quays and there is a significant rise and fall of tide you will need lines that are four times the range of the tide and these will be long. You just need to be careful.

The other day I asked a crewman at the bow how far I had to go before hitting the end of the berth. The call came back, 'About 1200 mil!'

'What? What's 1200mm, for heaven's sake?'

'About 4 feet.'

'Well, why didn't you say?'

In his defence he is a studio designer and so measures things in 'mils' rather than feet or yards.

Here's another thought: at your home berth, instead of the helm looking backwards as the boat approaches the dock stern-to, why not look forwards? Identify something fixed that will line up with something on

▲ Fender basket in line with post, in position.

## Specs saver

Ever lose your glasses? Not any more. Here's a neat idea: His, Hers and the Dog's baskets. Wallets, glasses, keys, phones stay in the baskets until needed. Now you always know where everything is – on board, that is. At home, we all still lose our glasses.

Guess which one belongs to the dog?

the boat when you are in the perfect position in your berth. All you do is drive astern until these two things are in line and you know you are in the right place in the berth. Sit at the helm and see what you can use. The post securing the finger pontoon is a good place to start. Does this line up with something like a stanchion when you are in the right spot? If so, that is what you will use. It doesn't help you in a foreign berth, but it is a really simple technique to use at your home berth.

## PREVAILING WIND

The wind is likely to come more often from one direction than any other. Choosing a berth where you are mostly blown on to the pontoon is probably preferable to one where you are being blown off, if you are short-handed. Be aware of where the wind comes from. In the UK, the weather and wind come more from the south-west than anywhere else. The lows track south-west to north-east. When the weather is fine, the wind will be from the north or thereabouts.

## Launching from trailers

**1.** Use a four-wheel-drive vehicle for towing.

**2.** Always have one other to help you.

**3.** Check that the slipway is suitable for launching your boat. Are there any tidal restrictions to launching?

**4.** When arriving at the slip, park up somewhere nearby to prep the boat. Don't do this on the slip as it may block others from launching their boats.

**5.** Check the hubs of the wheels of the trailer. If you have been travelling and they are hot, you have a bearing issue (salt water and bearings do not mix). Don't put the trailer into the water until it has cooled down as the heat will suck water into the bearing.

**6.** Brief your crew on the plan of action and don lifejackets.

**7.** Put the bung into the boat before launch.

**8.** Undo the safety straps but not the bow strap or safety chain at the bow.

**9.** Load your gear. Detach the plug for the brake lights and remove them from the stern of the boat.

**10.** Drive the boat down the slip until the stern just starts to float. Handbrake on and gear lever into park or in gear if manual and engine off.

**11.** Get on to the boat and lower the outboard.

**12.** Release the bow strap and safety chain.

**13.** Drive the boat off the trailer.

**14.** If the angle of the slip is shallow, remove the safety chain and ease off a couple of feet of the bow strap and lock this off on the winch before you drive the boat into the water. Then, as you drive the trailer into the water, and with the stern just about to float, tap the brakes. This will shunt the boat further along the trailer and make driving off under outboard that much easier.

**15.** If launching on soft sand, let down the tyres on the towing vehicle to about 20psi to make them softer and wider to stop them sinking in. Have a spade and a piece of wood ready to give a wheel grip if it gets stuck in a rut.

**16.** If the slip is very slippery, consider leaving the car on firm ground and lowering the trailer on a rope attached to the car.

**17.** Always carry a rope so someone can tow you out if your towing car gets stuck or so you can tow someone else out.

**18.** Before you set off for home, give the wheels, bearings and brake drums of the trailer a thorough wash off with fresh water. Don't wait until you get home. And grease the bearings regularly.

**19.** If the boat won't come off the trailer and if there is a pontoon by the slip, tie a line from the stern of the boat to a bollard on the dock. Now drive the car ahead up the ramp; this will pull the boat off the trailer a bit. Then drive the trailer back into the water and see if the boat will float off. Or push the boat off by hand.

**20.** Recovering the boat in a cross-current. Always drive into the tide. If you can jackknife the trailer so it is lining up with the tide, more or less, this will help. If this is not possible, hold the boat into the tide by the end of the trailer while the 'shore man' attaches the bow strap. Then, with a combination of winching in and driving ahead, it should be possible to swing the bow on to the trailer and drive the boat on. Alternatively, recover the boat at slack water if the slip is subject to strong tides.

Don't allow your thumb to go round the winch handle when gripping it. Keep your thumb on the outside of the handle so that you can pull your hand away quickly if necessary. And never, ever try to stop a spinning winch handle by hand!

# 6 GETTING OFF THE BERTH

Of all things to do with boating, getting off the berth and back on to it are the most stressful. I will have checked the forecast wind strength and direction, the tides and so forth before I left home. Then as I near the boat I will be looking at the trees and flags to see actual conditions. Will the wind be kind to me or will it drive me in the direction of my neighbour? I always know precisely what the tide is doing at any hour of the tide at my marina. And not all berths run fore and aft with the tide, occasionally one can be beam-on to the tide – that's the time to find another berth! That said, some berths can have the tide bouncing off the shore or creating awkward eddies. In any event, you will know exactly how the tide affects you at your home berth. The same applies to a river berth and the current.

If you find that there is nothing much to indicate the direction of the wind at your berth, look out for seagulls or other birds. When they perch they face the wind, as they will always take off into the wind.

How you get the boat off the dock rather depends on the number of crew and the size of the boat. Trying to get a 52ft Princess flybridge boat off the dock single-handed when it is being blown strongly off the pontoon is not going to be all that easy. There is going to come a time when you have to let go of whatever is holding you alongside, be it a spring or a bridle, and make your way to the saloon driving position or up to the flybridge, while the wind has a chance to blow you away from the dock. With a 28ft cabin cruiser you don't have so far to go from the

▲ Andy Hobbs, single-handing his 23M Princess. At slack water or a stand of the tide, he can take off the bow and stern lines and then the springs and hold the boat on the dock by using his remote control for the bow and stern thrusters.

point where you release the line to the helm position so this is going to be manageable single-handed.

In all the techniques I will show I will assume that you are short-handed – that is to say, you have one other crew. A partner perhaps? Occasionally you will be able to manage the technique single-handed. I should add that on all occasions when there is no wind or a gentle breeze blowing the boat on to the dock and pretty much slack water any boat can be single-handed off the dock. It is when there is a tide or a current and the boat is being blown off the dock that things become a little more challenging for the single-hander, and the bigger the boat the harder this can be. Yes, some have remote-control thrusters and can play their £2million investment like a radio-controlled toy, from the dock if they please, but this is the exception rather than the rule.

## FENDERING

First, though, you need to fender up well. A fender down to the water and up a bit is right for most pontoons. A fender taken under the lower guard rail or wire and over the upper guard rail on many boats up to 40ft becomes a fender at gunwale height, which is

▲ A fender down to the water and up a bit is generally right for most pontoons.

▲ Under the lower guard rail or wire and over the upper becomes a fender set at gunwale height without having to adjust the fender line.

ideal for rafting up or protecting yourself from a neighbour. This is a great shortcut if on arrival at your destination you suddenly have to change your fenders from pontoon height to gunwale height. You have

spotted a nice stretch of pontoon, but the harbour master or berthing master tells you that this last space in the harbour is reserved and that the only option for you is to raft up to another boat.

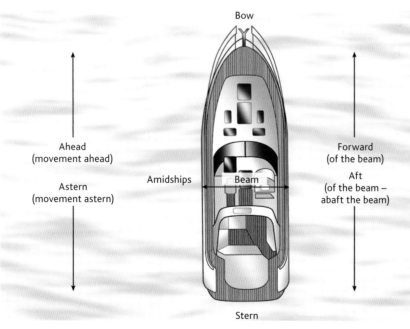

Ahead
(movement ahead)

Astern
(movement astern)

Amidships

Bow

Beam

Forward
(of the beam)

Aft
(of the beam –
abaft the beam)

Stern

▲ Parts of the boat and terms used.

## How many fenders?

I think four fenders either side is enough, with one on the stern if you are mooring stern-to. And if you're on a river and mooring to the bank, a bow fender to protect the boat as you drive it into the bank is a good idea.

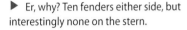
▶ Er, why? Ten fenders either side, but interestingly none on the stern.

**TOP TIP**

### Fender storage

Fender bungees are better than fender baskets. Here's a neat idea from Jonathan Parker of Sea Start: he has tied bungee cord to his guard rail. When the fenders are down, the bungees lie neatly between the lower wire and the guard rail, and when the fenders are on board, they are held captive by the bungees. Now there are no unsightly and bulky fender baskets on the side decks or foredeck.

Fender down, bungee out of the way, room to walk round the side deck.

Fender up, held in place by bungee.

# GRIP

Part of your preparation is establishing how much grip you will have on the water. As long as you have water travelling along the hull and over the rudder, you have grip. Say you have 1 knot of tide or stream. If you motor into this 1 knot at a speed through the water (our boat speed) of 2 knots you will have a speed of water over the hull of 2 knots and yet a speed over the ground of just 1 knot, because you are being pushed back by the tide or stream. You are in control.

However, if you go with the tide at a boat speed of 2 knots, you will again have a speed of water over the hull of 2 knots, but you will be travelling over the ground at 3 knots – our 2 knots plus 1 knot of tide – and you will be out of control. And this, of course, is why you always, always, always moor into the tide or stream.

The direction of the tide when it comes to exiting your berth is not as crucial as it is when you are mooring, but you do need to know what it will do to you so you can allow for this. It may be that the wind will have a greater effect on you than the tide as you manoeuvre out of the marina or the harbour or on the river. Whatever the case, you need to place the boat uptide or upwind at all times so you have a margin for error.

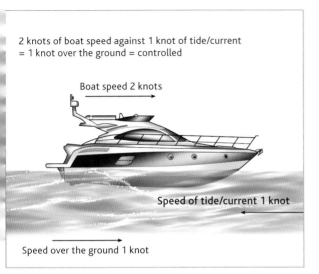

2 knots of boat speed against 1 knot of tide/current = 1 knot over the ground = controlled

Boat speed 2 knots

Speed of tide/current 1 knot

Speed over the ground 1 knot

▲ Controlled.

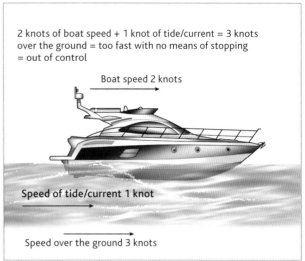

2 knots of boat speed + 1 knot of tide/current = 3 knots over the ground = too fast with no means of stopping = out of control

Boat speed 2 knots

Speed of tide/current 1 knot

Speed over the ground 3 knots

▲ Out of control.

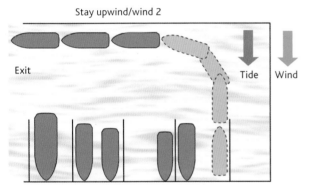

Stay upwind/wind 2

Exit

Tide | Wind

▲ Allowing for the tide or wind 1.

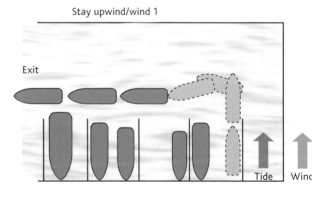

Stay upwind/wind 1

Exit

Tide | Wind

▲ Allowing for the tide or wind 2.

# EVERYTHING HANDLED FROM ON BOARD

I like to handle departure and arrival from on board, preferably from within the cockpit. Many boats, however, have ample bathing platforms with easier access to the stern cleats than from the cockpit, so you will often manage things from here.

However, if you are on the bathing platform I would advocate wearing a lifejacket and a lifeline. Many lifejackets for motorboaters have a plastic buckle and no 'D' ring so no immediately obvious attachment point for a lifeline. In this case, attach the lifeline directly to the harness and then attach the lifeline to a back rail on the transom. Now when the helm clicks the engine into ahead and everyone scuttles backwards, the crew on the bathing platform will not head immediately for the drink.

Many motorboats have the paraphernalia of the cockpit canopy frame and canvas precisely at the point that the crew need to be placed to manage the stern cleats. Often the ensign is positioned here.

That's easy: for the purposes of getting off the berth and getting back on, remove the ensign – and replace it

▲ Ensign in the way.

the minute you are off the dock. There is always a way of working round any obstruction and you just have to find a solution that suits you.

It is worth trying these techniques out on a wet Wednesday afternoon when hopefully no one else will be around. Remember, you always set up the technique while you are attached to the dock by your bow and stern lines and springs. Once you are confident that the technique is holding the boat against the dock you can start to lose the mooring lines.

## MOORING TERMINOLOGY

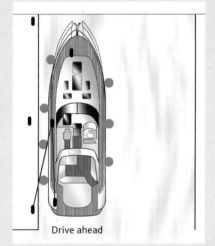
Drive ahead

▲ Spring.

**Spring** is a line that enters the boat at one point.

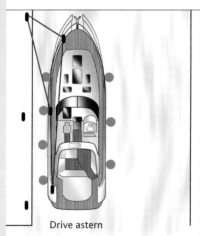
Drive astern

▲ Bridle.

**Bridle** is a line that enters the boat at two points.

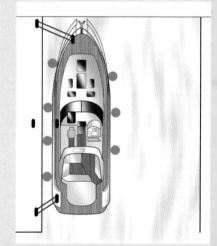

▲ Slipped lines.

**Slipped lines** are lines that go from the boat round something on shore and back to the boat and can be released from on board.

## Fixing the inboard end of a slipped line

In an ideal world you will have lines at your home berth that are set to the correct length for whatever you wish to do (see pre-made lines on page 72). This is part of the 'preparation'. It is much easier to have dedicated lines of good-quality rope at the right length than to use mooring warps for everything. But on the assumption that you are working with a line that is too long for the job in hand, to get the correct 'short' amount of line to release, you will have some spare line left over at the inboard end and will be attaching this end of the line part way down its length rather than at its end.

You can do this by OXOing the line on to a cleat (see Chapter 2). But if you are going to OXO the slipped end of the line to the same cleat (and you will probably have to do this as there may be only one stern cleat on each side of the boat), this may become bulky on the cleat.

Frankly the easiest thing to do is to tie a knot in the line – an overhand knot. The purists will object, but it will do the job. Set the

amount of line you need to go from the cleat on board to the shore cleat and back so you can slip the line. And assuming that you have a lot of line left over, double this line at this point and tie an overhand knot in it. The loop you create can then slip over the cleat. Take the spare line and run it to the cockpit or on deck, anywhere that keeps it tidy and out of the way of the line you have set to slip.

If you want to impress the chaps at the club you have three options:

**1 Tie a bowline in a doubled line**. You have set the slipped end of the line and now you have the inboard end of the line, the fixed end, the end you want to fix to the cleat. So double the line and make a bowline by forming a '6' (see Chapter 2).

**2 Tie an alpine butterfly knot** at the point you want the inboard end of the line to attach to the cleat (see Chapter 9).

**3 Tie a bowline on a bight**. This sounds much more complicated than it is. Again, you have set the slipped end of the line and now you have the inboard end of the

line, the fixed end, which you want to fix to the cleat. So double the line. Make a loop as if to make a bowline by forming a '6' (see Chapter 2). Now take the end of the loop (the running end, if you like) through this and then down over the loop of the bowline and up behind the rest of the knot. Pull on the loop of the bowline and the knot will form.

▲ Alpine butterfly knot.

▲ Bowline on a bight.

Scan the QR code to watch a video of tying an overhand knot into a doubled line, a bowline in a doubled line, an alpine butterfly knot and a bowline on a bight:

▲ Overhand knot tied into line to shorten it.

▲ Bowline in a doubled line.

## Slipping a long line

If you have a long line and you want to slip it without having to shorten it at the on-board end, then shorten it by taking a bight (a loop) round a cleat. You have to hold on to both ends until the line is slipped, but if you have crew this is something they can do. Or if you're single-handed and the line is long enough you can OXO it on board, until you are ready to slip it.

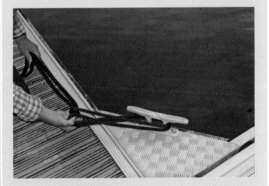

Around a cleat.

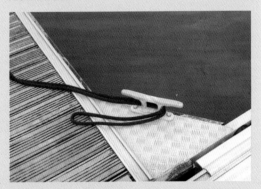

You can put the standing end through the bight. When releasing, haul in carefully to prevent the 'bight' (the doubled end) from catching on the cleat.

# FINGER BERTH

## Stern in

### 1. Slipped stern line

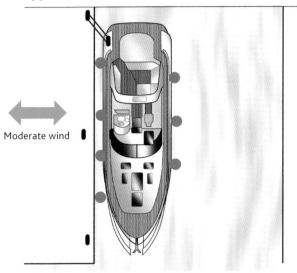

Moderate wind

▲ Stern in, driving ahead against a slipped stern line.

Here you are going to drive ahead against a slipped stern line. You start with the boat moored by a bow line, stern line and springs so that it is secured to the dock. Now if you have a line that is the right length for the job, all well and good. If not, you need to ensure that you have the least amount of line to slip. To do this, OXO temporarily on to the stern cleat the end of

▲ 42ft Sealine *Ramosseas* driving against a slipped stern line.

◀ Here, the 76ft *Lucky Ash* is being driven ahead against a slipped stern line. The line has been shortened by tying an alpine butterfly knot in it.

▲ Andy is handling the boat from the cockpit station. He will click the engine into neutral, release the slipped line, step up to the flybridge and drive off. He has the remote for the bow and stern thrusters round his neck.

the line that you will slip. Take the line to the shore, round the shore cleat and back to the boat. Take the temporary OXO of the slipped end off the cleat, and make your shortening knot (overhand, alpine butterfly, bowline on a bight etc.) in the on-board end of the line – the end that will be fixed to the boat. Place the loop this creates over the cleat. This is the inboard end, the end you will haul on. Then OXO the slipped end on top of this. You are ready. The helm should then click the engine into gear.

Twin-engined shaft-drive boats may find that using the inner engine will be best. Using the outer engine can cause the boat to start climbing the dock, depending on the power of the engines, of course. Stern-drive boats can adjust the rudder and prop to allow the boat to lie alongside comfortably. If there is a strong wind blowing the boat off the dock, then increasing the revs should keep it alongside.

With the boat holding alongside against the slipped stern line, you can remove the bow line, stern line and springs. Do these one at a time to make sure that the boat remains lying alongside nicely.

Remember at this point, or possibly before, to remove any shore power. Remove it from the shore end first so that if an end does go in the drink, it is not live.

If the boat is being blown strongly off the dock, you could add in a slipped bow line. This could run from the cockpit along the side deck to the bow, round the forward end of the bow cleat down to the cleat on shore, back up amidships and then along the side deck and back to the cockpit to be operated by the crew from the cockpit. Or you could set a slipped line from the bow to the shore and back, which the crew could release from the bow.

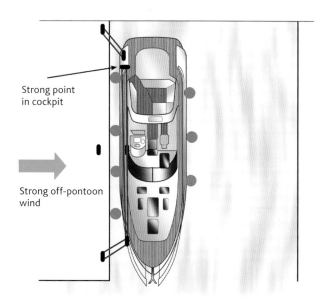

Strong point in cockpit

Strong off-pontoon wind

▲ Slipped stern line + slipped retaining bow line.

▲ This boat is holding alongside, driving against a slipped stern line with a retaining line for the bow to stop the bow being blown off. Note how the slipped end has the least amount of rope. The crew will release this first, then go to the stern, ask the helm to take the engine out of gear, then slip the stern line and the helm can drive the boat off the berth.

▲ *Tanzanite*, with stern drives, can vary the tension in the slipped stern line by increasing the astern propulsion on one of the engines so this can be eased when it is time to slip the line. Here the boat is running port engine ahead, starboard astern, which will turn it to starboard, and then with the helm to port to counter this. Net result: stern with no tension.

Generally, though, the power of the engine is sufficient to hold the boat alongside without having to use a retaining line for the bow.

You can leave the engine in gear throughout this on smaller boats (<35ft) – an OXO will undo under tension. But when it comes to the bigger boats (>35ft), such is the power of the engines that I think it is better to go

into neutral while the crew's fingers are releasing any OXOs. Check out the sort of tension you experience when driving against a slipped line, with the engine just clicked into ahead.

Stern-drive boats, of course, can adjust the tension on the line by having one engine in ahead and the other with a little helm in to angle the drive.

### Check your fixings  i

I have mentioned this in Chapter 5, but it bears repetition. Before you apply any load to a cleat or fixing on shore or on the boat, check that it is going to be up to the job. The same goes for any line that you will be using. You will not be putting any great strain on anything. And in any event you set up the spring or bridle with all the mooring lines set so that if anything were to go wrong, they would restrain the boat. Once you are comfortable that all cleats or fixings are fine as you drive against the line, you can remove the mooring warps.

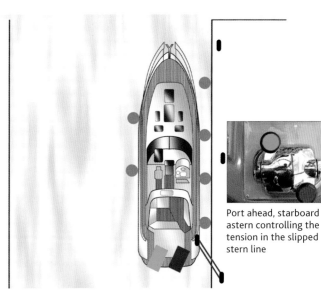

Port ahead, starboard astern controlling the tension in the slipped stern line

▲ Driving ahead against a slipped stern line.

## 2. Slipped stern bridle – stern in

If you have a wind blowing you off the dock, this is a useful technique as the boat is held alongside by the line coming on board at the midship cleat. You will be driving ahead against the stern part of the bridle and holding alongside by the midship part. Again, ensure that you have the least amount of line to slip.

To make sure of this, start with the slipped end by the stern cleat. Take the rest of the line forward along the side deck and then around the forward end of the midship cleat, outside everything to a cleat on shore by the stern and then back on board. Make this inboard end fast to the stern cleat (to make fast means to tie off). And then OXO the slipped end of the line on to this stern cleat as well.

You then click the engine in gear. Assuming the boat is holding alongside nicely, you can take the bow and stern lines and springs off. Even with a wind blowing strongly off the dock, the boat should hold alongside without the bow wandering off, as it is being held in two places, amidships and astern, by the bridle.

To depart, the helm clicks the engine into neutral, and the crew, on board, undoes the OXO on the slipped line and hauls steadily on the inboard end. With the boat free, the helm can drive off the dock. It may be possible on a smaller boat to leave the engine in gear while the crew slips line. An OXO will undo under tension – but be careful of crew's fingers when doing this.

Tide either way. Moderate to strong wind off the berth

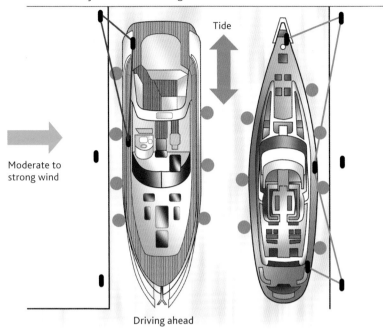

Moderate to strong wind

Tide

Driving ahead

▲ Driving ahead against a slipped stern bridle.

▶ Slipped stern bridle.

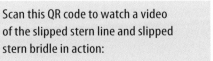 Scan this QR code to watch a video of the slipped stern line and slipped stern bridle in action:

### 3. Slipped bow bridle

You run this from a stern cleat, along the side deck to the bow, round the bow cleat to a cleat on shore by the bow, round this and back up amidships. Again, secure the inboard end of the line on the cleat and tidy away the spare. The slipped end is OXO'd on top. Click the engine into astern and the boat drives back against the bridle. Remove the mooring lines.

When you want to depart, you can either leave the engine in astern and then release the OXO of the slipped end and haul steadily in on the inboard end of the line, or ask the helm to put the engine into neutral while you do this. For twin-engined shaft-drive boats, using the inside engine only will probably be best, but check which engine in astern works best for your boat. Stern drives can, of course, adjust the helm to ensure the boat holds alongside nicely. Again, whether you leave the engine in gear as the crew release the slipped line will depend on engine power and tension in the line. If in doubt, put the engine into neutral to take the tension out of the line before the crew slip it.

Tide either way. Moderate wind blowing on/off or through

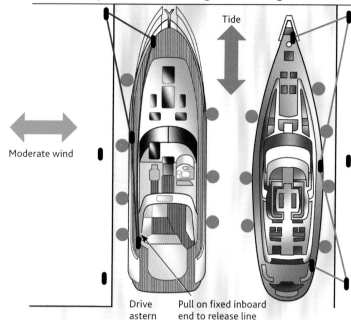

Moderate wind

Tide

Drive astern

Pull on fixed inboard end to release line

▲ Driving astern against a slipped bow bridle.

 Scan this QR code to watch a video of the bow bridle in action:

### Pre-made lines

You will probably use the same technique each time to come off your berth so it makes sense to make up lines specifically for the job. For coming off the dock and using slipped lines you want the lines to be the right length so you are not having to haul miles of line. You also want the lines to have an eye splice at the inboard end and nothing at the outboard end so that they can run free. You could use pre-made loops of line, but I prefer to use these for coming on to the dock rather than for getting off, just in case a loop cannot be detached from the shore for any reason.
A slipped line should always be able to slip free.

▲ Driving astern against the bow bridle. Make sure this is holding before taking off the mooring warps.

▲ Holding to the bow bridle, with mooring warps removed.

▲ Inboard end and outboard end of bridle OXO'd to a midship cleat.

▲ With engine in astern Alan takes the OXO off the cleat.

▲ Alan hauls in on the inboard end of the bridle.

▲ And he is off, all managed single-handed.

## 4. Slipped stern bridle – bow in

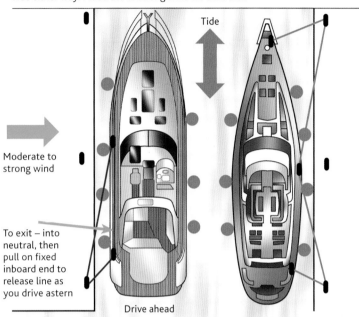

Tide either way. Moderate to strong wind off the berth

Tide

Moderate to
strong wind

To exit – into
neutral, then
pull on fixed
inboard end to
release line as
you drive astern

Drive ahead

▲ Driving ahead against a slipped stern bridle.

▲ Stern bridle set, driving ahead against this. Note inboard end of bridle bowlined on to cleat to leave room for the outboard end to be OXO'd on top.

Set this up exactly as you did for No. 2 and click the engine into ahead. One thing to remember with stern bridles is that the stern-most line will line up with the cleat or post on shore by the stern that the bridle is going round. If this means that your bow will be through the end of a finger pontoon, you need to set the point at which the line comes back on to the boat further forward. Again, twin-engined shaft-drive boats may find that using the inside engine works best,; stern drives will adjust the helm to suit. To depart, the helm will put the engine into neutral and the crew will release the bridle. When clear, the helm will drive astern to exit the berth.

You can always hold on to the dock against tide and wind (whether it is blowing you on or off) with a midship line. You can set it to slip by running the line from a stern cleat up to the midship cleat, through the centre part of this if there is one, down to the cleat on shore, back up to the midship cleat and around the front end of this and back to the stern cleat, where you make it fast. When you want to go, just slip it and drive off. This can be set up without the engine in gear. Motorboats being flat-sided, if you run a tight midship line then there will be very little give and very little chance that the bow or stern could move anywhere.

Setting lines to slip where they pass close to each other or through cleats, you need to make sure that you use nice slippery line. And also where possible, lead the two parts of the line different ways. The outboard end might go through the centre of a cleat and the inboard end round the forward part of the cleat. Being separated from one another reduces the friction from rubbing when hauling in.

Tide either way. Moderate wind on/off or through

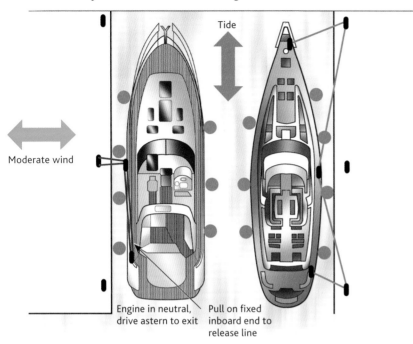

Tide

Moderate wind

Engine in neutral, drive astern to exit

Pull on fixed inboard end to release line

▲ Lying to a slipped midship line.

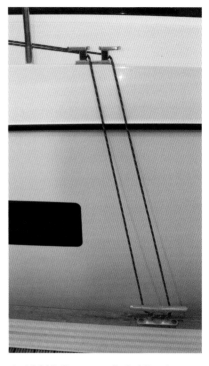

▲ Midship line set to slip, holding the boat close to the dock.

▲ Flat-sided motorboats can hang quite happily off a midship line. This line has not been led back to the cockpit.

▲ Parts of slipped line are separated so as to reduce friction.

# MEASURING WIND SPEED

Knowing the wind speed across the deck of your motorboat is incredibly important. Motorboats have a huge amount of windage, especially flybridge motorboats, and they have very little grip on the water. Even a deep V hull does not draw much water. Displacement boats, of course, are slightly better off than modern cruisers in that they have slightly less above the water and slightly more below, so less windage and more grip. But it is quite possible to find yourself on a flybridge boat being blown sideways across the water in any sort of reasonable wind on the beam. And you will find this happening to you just as you perform your slow manoeuvres, such as getting off the dock, getting on and picking up a mooring buoy. So it is a good idea to know where the wind is coming from and roughly how much there is.

## Handheld anemometer

An anemometer is a much more accurate way of establishing the speed and direction of the wind.

▲ Handheld anemometer.

## Windex

Look at the sailing boats and see what the wind instruments at the top of their masts are doing. The vane will give you the direction.

- If the cups of the anemometer are turning round lazily, there is no wind.

**TOP TIP**

## Always have a flag on the bow

A pennant or burgee on the pulpit will tell you which way the wind is blowing when you are travelling at low speed. It's handy to see what the wind will do to you when mooring. Make sure the pennant is made of flimsy material, light polyester is nice, so that it moves at the slightest breath of wind. A pennant that is too stiff doesn't really tell you a great deal.

Here's someone who has gone further and put a wind-indicating flag on his pulpit. This will be much more sensitive than a pennant or burgee.

- If you can see them spinning quite quickly, there is about 11–16 knots (Force 4).

- If you can't see the cups, there is a lot of wind: 25 knots plus (Force 6).

## Burgees and pennants

A **burgee** is a flag bearing the colours or emblem of a sailing club. It is usually triangular.

A **pennant** is a triangular flag. It may take the form of a burgee and represent a sailing club or it could simply bear the name of an organisation or business.

## Wind speed by flag

Or you can use a flag, an ensign say. This is very rough, but essentially:

- Flag hanging limp: wind speed below 10 knots (Force 3 and below)

- Flag flaps lightly and occasionally: wind speed 11–16 knots (Force 4)

- Flag flapping over the whole length of the flag: wind speed 17–21 knots

- Flag partially extended, flapping quickly: wind speed 22–27 knots (Force 6)

- Flag fully extended, flapping hard: wind speed 28–33 knots (Force 7) – stay in port!

Although, that said, the minute you crank the throttles up to warp speed, come up on the plane and watch the needles rise to 35 knots you are into Force 8, a full gale, and you have created this entirely on your own, regardless of the wind on the day.

# 7 GETTING ON TO THE BERTH

Now that you are off the dock, how are you going to get back on? There are a number of techniques you can use. All you have to do, one way or another, is to get a line to the dock and around a cleat so that you drive against that. First, though, you need to consider your approach.

## THE APPROACH

Always moor into the tide. Whether you are coming alongside a stretch of pontoon, coming into a dead-end finger berth, rafting up alongside another boat, coming up to a mooring buoy or mooring to a riverbank, always drive into the tide or current. If you are berthing 'bows in', drive ahead into the tide. If you are to be 'stern in', drive astern into the tide. The tide will usually be the dominant force on the boat.

Occasionally in a strong wind and slack water or little current, the wind will be the stronger force, but a quite modest flow of water will usually overpower the effect of the wind. However, not always, so you need to judge which has the greater effect on the boat. I have a berth where the prevailing wind blows through and has a significant effect on the boat, and requires quite a strong tide to overcome it.

Also consider the effect of a crosswind. As long as you have some 'way' on and a grip on the water you should be able to counter any crosswind, although your ability to do this will depend on your hull design and the profile your boat presents to the wind, your windage. Many motorboats have very little grip on the water as a result of their hull shape and yet present a

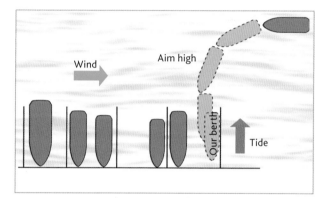

▲ Approach 1.

large area above the water for the wind to work on. They are susceptible to being swept sideways, which is always disconcerting. You just have to be aware of this and allow for it.

If you are being blown on to the berth, aim high (to windward), and use the wind to blow you into your berth. If you've misjudged and are a little to windward of the berth, then it is just a matter of waiting as the wind blows you on. The one thing you don't want to do is aim at your berth, because as the wind blows on you it will push you downwind of your berth and you will miss. If this happens, back out of the manoeuvre and start again.

If you are being blown away from your berth, you could again aim high (to windward) and allow the wind to blow you into the gap, although doing this you risk being blown on to your neighbour or being blown past the berth and having to bail out of the exercise. It's preferable to approach the berth at an angle: go past the berth, turn back up into the wind and drive in. Then you have control.

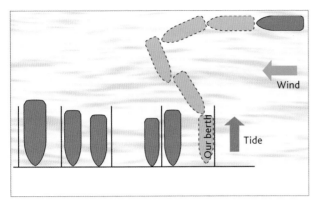

▲ Approach 2.

If you are short-handed (i.e. if it is you and one crew) then one person can man the helm and the other can handle the ropework. Most important here is to remember that the helmsman should never leave the helm. If the crew has missed when they tried to get a line ashore, or something has gone wrong, there is the temptation to leave the helm and help. Now what you have is a boat that is not attached to the shore and not being controlled by the helm; this is highly undesirable. As frustrating as it might be, the helmsman must remain at the helm and control the boat until the crew is ready to try again.

## FERRY GLIDING

You can also use the tide or current to move the boat sideways and help you moor. This technique is used by everyone from large passenger ships to small canoes and kayaks. Let's say you have a tide of one knot on the bow. You can hold the boat stationary over the ground by driving into the tide at one knot. You will have a boat speed taking you forward through the water of one knot, so with the tide running at one knot in the opposite direction, you will actually be stationary.

Now you want to go sideways so you turn your bow to bring the flow of water on to one side or the other. The stronger the flow the smaller you make this angle on the bow. As you drive forward, stemming the flow, you will be moved sideways. This is called ferry gliding and is a very useful technique to have up your sleeve. In actual fact, most motorboats will have to click the engines in and out of gear to achieve this as their idle speed will be greater than that of the tide.

To use ferry gliding to help you berth, arrive at the pontoon a little way off, turn your bow into the tide, drive against this and get pushed sideways to the pontoon or berth. Just before you arrive, straighten the boat up and come alongside perfectly. Check this out on a wet Wednesday afternoon, with plenty of space and plenty of fenders.

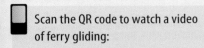 Scan the QR code to watch a video of ferry gliding:

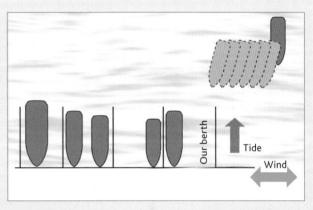

▲ Ferry gliding.

▲ *Le Coq* ferry gliding.

Note that you manage all these techniques from on board the boat. You don't step off until the boat is holding alongside, driving against a bridle.

Another point to make is that it is the helm's job to get the boat to the dock – any bit will do. It is the crew's job to attach the line that the helm can drive against to hold the boat alongside. It is not the crew's job to make up for poor helmsmanship.

## Approaching bows first

### 1. Stern bridle

This is an excellent technique for mooring up to a stretch of pontoon or a finger berth, because even if conditions mean that you are unable to get close to the pontoon you should be able to lasso a cleat. With a few coils of line in each hand, even a fairly weak throw should manage to send the line a good five feet. So if you are closer to the pontoon than this, say three feet off, you will be able to get that crucial line ashore. And three feet off the dock is some way off – a massive miss in berthing terms. You would hope to be able to get closer than this. Of course, practising lassoing is key.

With the line around a shore cleat, simply drive the boat gently against this to bring it alongside. This

**TOP TIP**

### Brief the crew

The helm never leaves his position. However frustrating it is to watch crew who are not getting it quite right, he must resist the temptation to join them. He can be more useful at the helm. He can control the boat. Out on deck he cannot control the boat. Which is why it is so important to communicate with crew before any manoeuvre so everyone understands what is going to happen. And crew, in turn, need to prepare things in advance so that the chances of them executing their part of the exercise correctly will be improved.

is my preferred technique for berthing, whether bows in or stern in, because being a bridle, it pins the boat at two points, amidships and the stern. And this will help to counter the effect of a wind blowing the boat off the dock, without having to increase revs on the engine beyond tickover. Remember you are not using this bridle to stop the boat; you should slow the boat to a standstill before lassoing the cleat.

Set this up as follows:

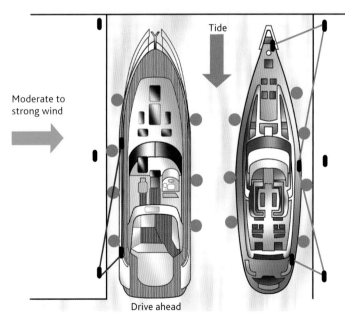

Tide

Moderate to strong wind

Drive ahead

▲ Bows first: stern bridle set up.

**1** Make a line fast to a midship cleat. If you are OXOing the line to the cleat, add in a locking hitch for safety. You could always attach the line with a bowline.

**2** Lead the line outside everything and bring it back inboard at a stern cleat. Take the line through the centre of the cleat if possible. This will stop it falling into the drink.

**3** Now pull through the stern cleat enough line to make four coils for the lasso without allowing that part of the line from you to the midship cleat to fall into the drink.

**4** When the helm has stopped the boat alongside the chosen cleat, lasso it by flicking the line high and wide.

**5** Then haul in steadily to tighten the bridle, making sure you do not pull the line off the cleat or bollard.

**6** Make the bridle fast with an OXO and locking hitch on the stern cleat.

**7** Ask the helm to put the engine in gear ahead and the boat will drive against the bridle.

## BOWS FIRST: STERN BRIDLE

▲ Line of bridle through centre of cleat to keep it safe.

▲ Notice that the bridle is secured to the midship cleat with an OXO led back to and through the centre of the stern cleat, and that four coils are ready to lasso.

◀ Time to lasso.

▲ Tightening the bridle.

▲ Making the bridle fast; holding alongside under engine.

It is important when you're driving against a bridle to keep the engine in gear all the time. There were a couple of occasions when setting up the shots when I found the boat drifting off the dock because the helm had taken the engine out of gear. The boat came back alongside nicely when the engine was put back into gear, of course.

With the boat now driving against the bridle and holding alongside, you have two options:

**1** Step off and set the bow line and springs and then take the engine out of gear.

**2** If the bow is accessible via the side decks or through a gate in the windscreen, you can take the bow line and lasso the cleat on shore. In reality, you just drop the line over the cleat. Then, with a bow line and stern bridle attached, you can take the engine out of gear, step ashore, release the stern bridle and set a proper stern line and then the springs.

On bigger boats this is the system I prefer. Everything is managed on board before you step off. You could even set the springs from on board. Tie a bowline in the end of a line and drop this over a cleat amidships on the shore before making it fast, then tie a bowline in a second line and drop this over that same cleat on shore. Now make one line fast at the bow and the other at the stern and that's your springs done. You can adjust all lines later. But for now you have bow line, stern line and springs attached to the shore from on board.

On some boats where there is a support for the flybridge aft, it is not easy to set up the bridle. On *Ramosseas* we tie a bowline to the end of the bridle that will go round the midship cleat and hang this on a convenient hook that can be reached from the side deck. We keep the line on the bathing platform tidy until we are ready to set this up, by wrapping it over a rail on the transom.

▲ Andy lassoing the cleat on shore for the bow line.

▲ Bowline to attach the bridle to the midship cleat ready for crew to collect from the side deck.

▲ Spare line for bridle wrapped on transom rail.

▲ Cleat lassoed, aft end of bridle made fast on aft cleat and inside engine clicked into gear and driving against the stern bridle, holding the boat alongside.

Scan the QR code for a video of the stern spring, stern bridle and midships line techniques in action:

## Measuring up

When you're coming into a finger berth it is most important to check that, once you have lassoed the cleat at the end of the pontoon (the first one you come to as you enter the berth), the boat will stop before it digs its bows into the end of the berth. You can measure all this on your berth before you set off.

Wherever you bring the sternmost part of the bridle back on board will line up with the cleat you have lassoed on shore. If this leaves your bow four feet through the pontoon at the end, you need to think again. You need either a longer berth or to find a point further forward on the boat to bring the sternmost part of the bridle back on board. Motorboats are not blessed with multiple cleats at the forward end of the cockpit, so you might have to be inventive.

As motorboaters, we are not awfully impressed by lots of string and these few bridles that I have suggested are quite enough to be working with, but if you had to improvise a secure point through which to return the sternmost part of the bridle, I'd suggest getting a short line made up with an eye splice in one end to loop over the midship cleat. You could have a ring spliced into the other end, a rubber one so as not to damage the side decks.

Now with the line looped around the midship cleat and coming down the side deck, with the ring in line with the cleat on shore, which allows you to stop in your berth before hitting the end, run the sternmost part of the bridle through the ring and secure on the aft cleat. You have now moved the sternmost return of your bridle on board forward. You could test this out or even run this by using any line, attaching one end to the midship cleat and then tying a bowline in the other end at the point you need to stop the boat.

With your bridle attached to the midship cleat, going outside everything and back to a stern cleat or your sternmost point to get into the berth, make four coils for the lasso and separate them to leave two coils in either hand, with one piece of line connecting them. It is worth taking a turn round the stern cleat with the remainder of the line so you don't lose it.

As the helm gets you alongside and stopped by what you will be lassoing on shore, be it a cleat or a post, throw or drop the line over and then haul in the slack and make fast on the cleat with an OXO. With our stern bridle in place and tight, the helm can click the engine into gear and the boat will remain alongside. It is only then that you step off to set the bow line, stern line and springs. With these in place, take the engine out of gear and retrieve the line for the bridle.

## 2. Stern line

When approaching a length of pontoon, the helm will get the boat alongside and stopped and you will lasso a cleat on the pontoon and make the inboard end fast, and then the helm will click the engine in gear (inner engine for a twin-engined boat) and the boat will lie alongside held by the stern line.

Set this up by attaching one end of a line to a stern cleat, making four coils, holding two in either hand, lassoing the onshore cleat and then tightening the line and making it fast to the stern cleat. Again, once the line is secure, the helm will click the engine into ahead and keep it there so that the boat holds alongside, driving against the stern line.

## 3. Midship line

This is a line you will run from your midship cleat, down to a cleat on shore and then back up to the midship cleat. Again, make four coils, two in either hand, and when the helm has brought you alongside the cleat on shore, drop the coils over the cleat. Be careful when hauling in that you don't bring the line back over the top of the cleat as you will be lassoing from above. With the line under both wings of the cleat on shore, harden up and make it fast to the midship cleat on board. Now the boat can't go anywhere and you can take the engine out of gear.

▲ Coils in hand ready to lasso the cleat.

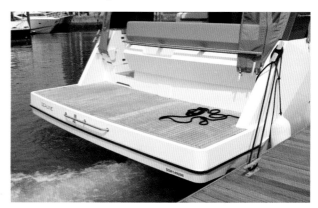

▲ Cleat lassoed, line OXO'd back on board, boat driving ahead against line on inner engine, lying alongside nicely.

▲ Coils ready to lasso.

## PRE-MEASURED STERN LINE

Here is a pre-made loop for the stern line in action. The two ends of the line have been tied with a double fisherman's knot. Rebecca can just drop this over the cleat and slip the other end round the stern cleat on board, Jonathan can then click the engine into ahead, and that's it.

**TOP TIP**

### Use a fender, not your body

Always place a fender between your boat and any impending accident. Do not place any part of you between the two, especially not hands, and do not push on the guard rail of any boat as this could bend it. It is acceptable on smaller boats to hold or push them by a stanchion, but you must push the base of the stanchion.

▲ Pre-made loop of line.

▲ Place around cleat on shore.

▲ Then round cleat on board.

▲ Alongside, driving against the stern line.

▲ Cleat lassoed.

▲ Tight midship line, this boat is not going anywhere.

# Approaching stern first

## 1. Stern line

Here you can lasso a cleat on the dock by the stern and drive ahead against this as for No. 2 on page 84.

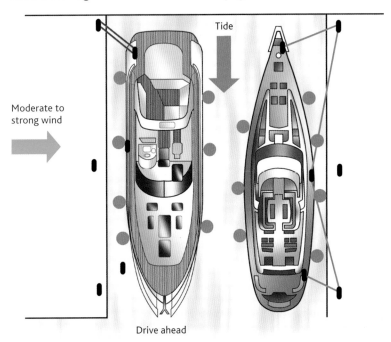

▲ Getting on stern in, with a stern line.

▲ Cleat lassoed, holding the boat alongside with inside engine clicked into ahead.

## 2. Stern bridle

Set up a stern bridle and lasso a cleat on the dock by the stern and drive ahead against this. This will help to hold the bow in, because of the bridle running from amidships and the stern. Useful on a day when the wind is blowing you strongly off the pontoon.

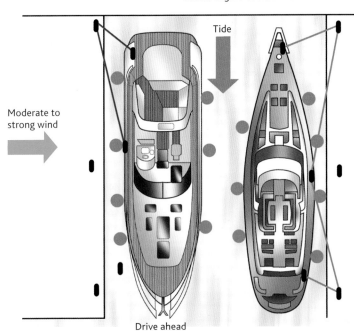

▶ Getting on stern in, with a stern bridle.

# RING MOORINGS OR HOOPED CLEATS

How do you get on to ring moorings? This will be tricky if you come across them at a foreign marina, but if they are what you have at your home berth, you can prepare for them (see Chapter 5).

If you find rings on a finger berth you might be able to lasso the entire end of the finger. That works for short wobbly French fingers as well. This is the case only if there is no boat on the other side of the finger as its stern line will stop you from doing this. There might be no alternative but to back into the space, stern-to, step off and feed a line through the ring, take this back to the boat and make fast.

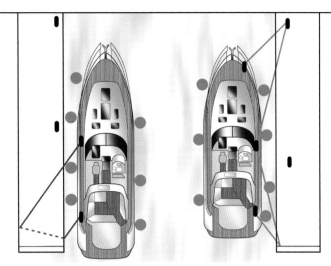

▲ Short thin fingers with no cleats: again, lasso the entire finger.

▲ Rings: lasso the entire finger.

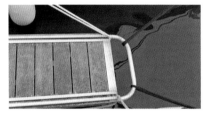

▲ You can lasso the finger, unless there is someone moored on the other side!

---

## MCA position on motoring against springs

I am mindful that I should be advising 'safe practice', so I contacted the Maritime Coastguard Agency in January 2014 to ask them if they had a view on motoring against springs, or if they had ever made any ruling about this, and this is what they told me:

*'The MCA's surveyors are seafarers who apply their maritime knowledge to identify potential problems before they happen. They have never ruled that powering against a spring was unsafe and illegal; indeed they recognise the process of using a vessel's engine in combination with a suitably positioned spring is an appropriate way of berthing a vessel; however, there is a difference between berthing a vessel and boarding passengers. The MCA has stopped vessels powering against a single line while passengers are getting on and off to protect those who may not have any nautical knowledge or whose mobility may be impaired.'*

And they hold this view because they are the accountable authority.

You will notice that when you get on a passenger ferry, they still power against a spring but have a second line attached to the shore as back-up. This no doubt covers them against the line in the MCA rule above ('powering against a single line while passengers are getting on and off').

Remember that you are not using any of these techniques to stop the boat. The boat should be stationary or very nearly so when you attach yourself to the dock. You arrive, you get the bridle line or spring ashore, you drive against this until the boat is alongside, then you step ashore, moor the boat properly and then take the engine out of gear.

▲ I assume these four are all friends and have agreed that if the outer boat sets shore lines, that will be sufficient. Normally each boat would set lines to the shore.

**TOP TIP**

## No more sleepless nights

Old mooring warps tend to creak as they come under tension and this can be very irritating, especially at night. Once the warps start doing this it's time to renew them. However, any rope can make a dreadful creaking sound if it is rubbing against a toe rail, but if you put a plastic bag between the rope and the toe rail the creaking disappears. It looks a bit weird, but it works.

Fridges that hum, bang and whirr in the night? Turn them off! And just when you have done that and gone back to sleep there will be an almighty crash as the ice maker in the cockpit deposits fresh cubes into the bin. You might as well turn that off as well. Who needs ice in the middle of the night? I prefer sleep.

◀ Of course, you could drive very fast at the dock and get your boat entirely out of the water. Drive on the floating dock, quite the fashion these days.

## RAFTING UP

The key to rafting up is to get a centre line from you to the host boat as soon as you are alongside. This short line will prevent you from being pushed back with the tide or wind. You will have arrived alongside motoring into the tide, with fenders set at gunwale height. The host boat may also have fenders set at gunwale height, but even if they have, you need to have yours set, too.

The correct procedure as you draw close to them is to hail them by boat name and ask permission to raft alongside. If there is no one on board, just carry on.

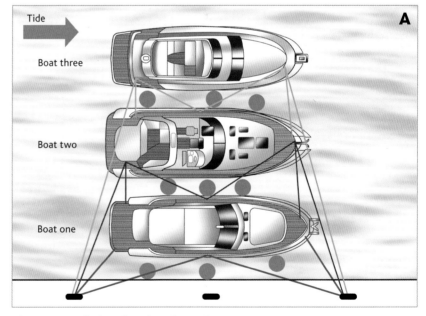

▲ How to set the lines for a three-boat raft.

If there is someone on board, they may welcome you with 'We are leaving at four in the morning.' This is probably a ploy to get you to raft up somewhere else. Invariably I find I have left before them in the morning.

The next thing is that they will be keen to take your lines. Do not be tempted to hand them any lines, simply tie off a very short line between the two boats amidships. With this attached you won't be going anywhere and can set your lines at leisure. (I am not fond of handing a stranger a line and relying on their ability to attach it securely. I'm not being fussy, I am sure they would feel the same.) Tie a bowline in the end of a line and hand it to their crew to loop over a cleat on their boat. You will then lead the line back to your boat and make the adjustments on board your boat. This applies to the bow line, stern line and springs. You will then need to run shore lines.

## Leaving from the middle of a raft

Occasionally there will be someone in the middle of the raft who would like to leave before those outside them. This is great because everyone comes together as a team to do this so there is very little tutting and generally everyone is good-humoured about it.

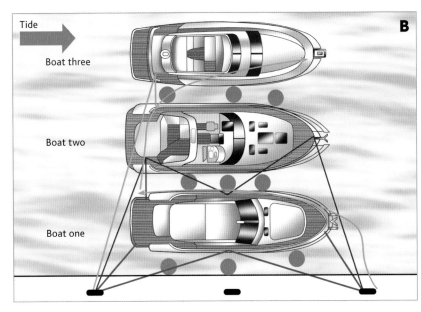

▲ Lines set to allow the middle boat to leave.

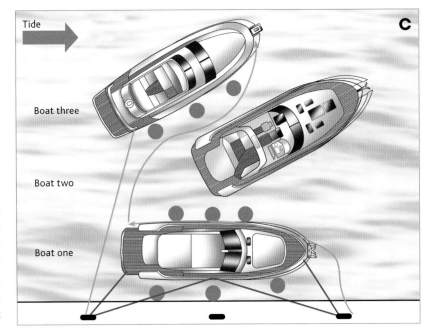

▲ The outer boat is then brought alongside with her shore lines.

One option is for outside boats to un-raft themselves, stooge about until the leaving boat has gone and then raft up again.

Another option is to open out a raft. You need to prepare for this. Always open out a raft downtide, never with the tide. You don't want the tide splitting the raft apart. That could end in disaster. If you are downtide, the tide will be pushing the raft back together, which will help once the inside boat has gone.

# 8 MOORING BUOYS

Traditionally the business of picking up a mooring buoy has involved the crew heading for the foredeck and trying to guide the helm to the buoy.

And on a small boat with no side decks, this will still be the way to do it.

On bigger boats the helm up on the flybridge loses sight of the buoy as the boat closes with it, and they often cannot hear what the crew, some 20 feet away and facing the buoy, are saying. Worse, the helm may be inside, as in the case of a sports cruiser. All in all, it is something of a communication nightmare.

The crew are unable to give meaningful signals as they will have the boathook in one hand and will be hanging on to the guard rail while the deck bounces up and down beneath them. The foredeck of a motorboat is not a great place to be, especially if there is any swell. Also there is little comfort to be gained from the pulpit, which often extends out over the bow at an awkward angle. Not ideal for leaning on. So let's not go there. I don't like the crew being out on the foredeck deck, unless there is no other option.

## PICKING UP THE BUOY FROM ALONGSIDE

I prefer crew to manage everything from the cockpit or, if this is not possible, to be positioned more or less amidships. Here there will be a coachroof, with perhaps a rail to hang on to, as well as the guard rail. They can even sit on the coachroof just in front of the screen until the helm has the buoy alongside.

And you will pick up the buoy amidships, or from alongside the cockpit. There is a good chance that the helm will be able to see the buoy pretty much up to the last moment, possibly all the way on a flybridge boat if he is able to bring the buoy to the side on which the helm is positioned. And crew and helm are near each other and can hear one another. The crew can, of course, point the boathook at the buoy to help the helm if he loses sight of it.

## TYPES OF BUOY

There are two types of buoy:

**1** Those with a pendant with an eye splice in the end and a pick-up float, which you can grab with a boathook.

**2** Those with nothing in the top except a ring, a bar or a shackle, which you will have to lasso.

▲ Moorings.

▲ Mooring buoy with pendant, eye in pendant, pick-up line and pick-up float.

▲ Mooring buoy with iron shackle.

▲ Mooring buoy with its own bow wave.

Actually there is also a third type of buoy, and this is buoy No. 2 when there is a strong tide running. Now the buoy will have its own bow wave or be awash, and if you lasso this with a normal rope you will just get it thrown straight back at you. You will need a heavy-duty, weighted lasso to get a line over the buoy.

## APPROACH AND PICK-UP

Let's look at picking up buoy No. 1, the one with a pendant, eye splice and pick-up float.

Rather than pick up the pendant and walk it to the bow, which means for part of the time the crew is a human cleat between boat and buoy, get some rope to do the work.

Run a bridle from the buoy to amidships or to the stern, if you are picking it up from the cockpit. Then pick out the pendant, put down the boathook, thread the bridle through the eye, secure the bridle to a cleat and wait. The boat will be attached to the buoy and drift back with the tide, because you always moor into the tide, and the buoy will make its way to the bow. Now safely moored, you can go forward and attach the pendant to a cleat.

To set this up:

Run a line from the bow cleat opposite the side on which you will pick up the buoy. If you attached it to the same side as the one on which you will pick up the buoy, you'd find it very difficult to remove the line once you had slipped the pendant eye splice over the cleat. If there is just a line running through the centre of the cleat or past the cleat it is easy to pull through.

Then store the line, either on a cleat with an OXO or tied to the guard rail with a rustler's hitch (see Chapter 2) in readiness.

▲ Bow bridle attached to starboard cleat and passing in front of port cleat. The buoy will be picked up on port.

▲ Bow bridle attached to port cleat with an OXO. It would be impossible to release this if you had the eye of a pendant on the cleat on top of this. That's why you set the bridle from the side opposite that on which you will pick up the buoy.

The helm approaches from downtide and to leeward of the buoy, in an ideal world.

However, if there is any breeze, most motorboats will be blown around a great deal – lots up top and not much in the water – so it is necessary to find an approach that keeps windage to a minimum. Putting the stern into the wind is the only answer. If you have the bow to the wind it will get blown off, and if you are beam-on to the wind, no engines or combination of engines and thrusters can really counter the effect of the wind.

Try to approach from downtide, if not necessarily from directly downtide. It may be necessary to approach from uptide if that is where the wind is coming from. Obviously care has to be taken to make sure that you don't overrun the buoy. Remember, you are not running directly down on to the buoy – you are coming alongside it. However, if it looks as if this manoeuvre will be difficult to manage (and you will know this by testing it out in a bit of open water before approaching the buoy, just to check that you have the control you need), then, discretion being the better part of valour, move on to Chapter 9 and find a spot to anchor.

### 1. Crosswind as you face into the tide

See Diagram 1.

You will stand off, get a feel of the strength of the tide and the wind and then turn up towards the buoy from its windward side, with the wind on your stern. Now the effect of windage is significantly reduced. It will not blow the boat sideways, it will push it along, but you can control this with a blip of astern as necessary.

Once you have the bridle on the buoy you can line yourself up with the tide. Single-engined boats will put the helm hard aport and give a burst of power off the rudder. Twin-engined boats will put the starboard engine into ahead and the port engine into astern.

### 2. Wind on the shoulder as you face into the tide

See Diagram 2.

### 3. Wind on the quarter as you face into the tide

See Diagram 3.

### 4. Wind on the nose as you face into the tide

See Diagram 4.

Once you are attached to the buoy you need to turn the boat so the bow is facing into the tide and the wind.

Single-engined boats go astern. Prop walk will take the stern one way or another and the wind and tide will push the boat round. Keep in astern so as not to be run down on to the buoy.

Twin-engined boats click either engine, but not both, into astern. The outer engine always tucks the stern into the dock with its prop walk. The same will happen here. From Diagram 4, port engine astern will take the stern to starboard, and vice versa for the starboard engine. As the wind and tide catch the boat, try to control the swing in order not to put too much strain on the mooring buoy and its sinker.

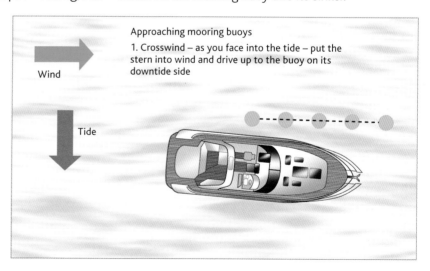

Approaching mooring buoys

1. Crosswind – as you face into the tide – put the stern into wind and drive up to the buoy on its downtide side

Wind

Tide

▶ Diagram 1.

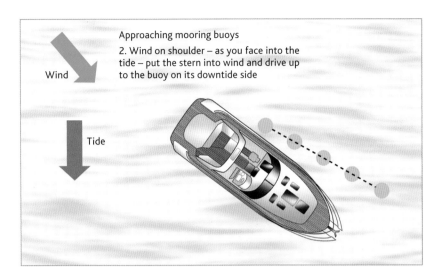

Approaching mooring buoys

2. Wind on shoulder – as you face into the tide – put the stern into wind and drive up to the buoy on its downtide side

Wind

Tide

▶ Diagram 2.

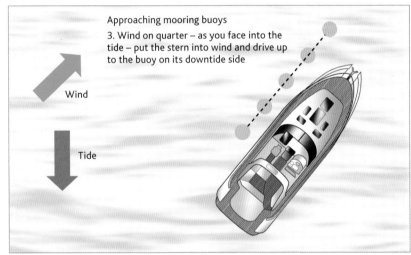

Approaching mooring buoys

3. Wind on quarter – as you face into the tide – put the stern into wind and drive up to the buoy on its downtide side

Wind

Tide

▶ Diagram 3.

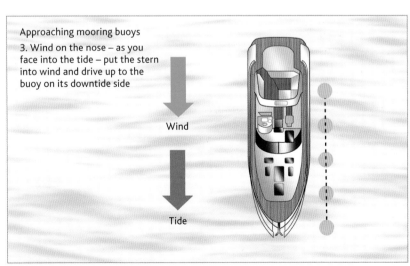

Approaching mooring buoys

3. Wind on the nose – as you face into the tide – put the stern into wind and drive up to the buoy on its downtide side

Wind

Tide

▶ Diagram 4.

## PICKING UP A BUOY WITH A PENDANT AND PICK-UP FLOAT FROM AMIDSHIPS ON A 32FT SPORTS CRUISER

▲ The helm brings the buoy alongside. Note how Rebecca has tied the bridle to the guard rail with a rustler's hitch so that it is safe and yet she can get it easily. When you're picking up a buoy amidships no bow bridle should be long enough to reach back to the propellers of the boat.

▲ Hooked.

▲ The eye of the pendant in hand, ready to grab the bow bridle with a quick flick of the rustler's hitch instant-release knot.

▲ And thread it through the eye.

▲ Bow bridle OXO'd on to the midship cleat. The buoy makes its way to the bow.

▲ That's it.

■ Rebecca is in communication with Jonathan on the helm throughout the manoeuvre.

# PICKING UP A BUOY WITH A PENDANT FROM THE COCKPIT IN A 50FT FLYBRIDGE BOAT

▲ Buoy alongside.

▲ Grabbed with the boathook.

▲ On board.

▲ Bridle through the eye of the pendant.

▲ And OXO'd on to the stern cleat.

▲ The buoy makes its way to the bow.

▲ Done.

▲ Notice how the bow bridle has been led through the centre of the cleat to stop it sliding along the gunwhale and putting any strain on any of the stanchions.

The next issue you have is: how far from the water is the deck? On some boats, even an extended boathook is not long enough to pick anything out of the water.

Generally I'd say that mooring buoys with pendants, eye splices and pick-up floats should be grabbed by a boathook and that mooring buoys with nothing but an iron ring or shackle in the top should be lassoed. But on big boats where it is impossible to reach down, all buoys need to be lassoed.

▶ The boathook does not reach down to the water. To pick up a float Jo-Ann would have to lean right out and it would have to be right beside the boat.

## PICKING UP A MOORING BUOY WITH A LASSO FROM AMIDSHIPS IN A 42FT FLYBRIDGE BOAT

▲ Bringing the boat alongside.

▲ Four coils at the ready.

▲ Lassoing high and wide does it.

▲ Jo-Ann walks to the bow as the boat slips back…

▲ and OXOs the lasso to the bow cleat. Moored.

## Lassoing with both ends of the lasso tied to the boat

The advantage of picking up a buoy alongside is that the helm knows that the buoy will remain on that side. When you're picking up from dead on the bow the buoy often slips from one side to the other and the helm is unaware of what is happening.

You don't have to hold the boat alongside the buoy for very long, just long enough for the crew to grab it, be it with a boathook or a lasso.

On smaller boats you might pick up the buoy using a long line with a snap shackle on the end.

▲ Rebecca is ready with her three coils. Both ends of the lasso are attached to the boat.

▲ With the buoy lassoed, she can let go. The lasso being a loop, the boat is attached to the buoy.

## PICKING UP A BUOY WITH A LONG LINE

▶ Buoy with pendant and pick-up float.

▶▶ Thread the line through the eye of the pendant and clip the snap shackle back on the standing part of the line…

▶ and haul in until you are beside the buoy.

## Approach and control of the boat

I have talked about what may or may not be possible with different boats and you will know how your boat behaves. It is a good idea to stand off the mooring buoy and check that the position and angle you aim to pick up the buoy from will work, given the wind and tide at the time. And that you can hold the boat by the buoy for just long enough to allow the crew to attach the boat to the buoy.

As you'll be running past the buoy if you pick it up amidships or by the cockpit, make sure there is room ahead. On a run of buoys there will be other boats moored so you need to find a buoy where there will be sufficient space for you to employ your technique.

## Boathooks cannot be released under tension

Getting a boathook into the hand grip of a small buoy or through a metal hoop is all very well. You draw what you have hooked towards you and remove the boathook. But if there is any tension on the hook (say you have hooked successfully and now you and the boat are drifting away from the buoy), you will not be able to release the boathook.

You can try twisting the boathook and the hook may release, but the only real way to resolve this is for the tension to be released by the helm getting the boat back to the buoy or by you letting go of the boathook before your arms are wrenched from their sockets.

And now, not only are you not moored to the buoy, you have a boathook in the drink and you have lost your means of mooring to the buoy.

Which is why the cautious will have prepared a slip knot, so that they can hoik the boathook out of the drink (see Chapter 2).

## Devices

There are a number of mooring devices (Hook and Moor, Moorfast, Seamark Nunn, Got it! Mooring Catcher etc.). If they are big enough to go round the ring or shackle and man enough for the job these are fine. I prefer to use rope, but I have seen some excellent devices and you may prefer to use one of these. Lassoing generally is man enough for anything.

## Lassoing a buoy

If you find that you are above the buoy as you lasso it, rather than a few feet away, make sure you wait a moment for the line to sink below the buoy before applying any pull.

Ideally you want to be a few feet away from the buoy to have a lateral element of pull. You want the line around the chain to be below the buoy. If it is still on the buoy it may slip off the top.

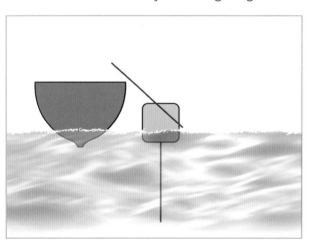

▲ Too close – the pull is too vertical – the lasso is apt to come off.

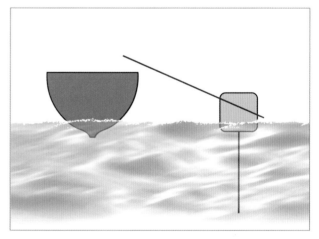

▲ The right distance – the pull is lateral – the lasso will catch the buoy.

## Use your mobiles to communicate

Communication about the boat? Even from the flybridge to the cockpit, where there is quite a bit of engine noise, it can be difficult to hear what is being said. There are walkie-talkie headsets available, marketed as 'Marriage Savers'! But how about using a mobile phone? Both the helm and the crew can be hands-free on earpieces. You will be close to shore so you should have a mobile signal.

Don't forget when lassoing that you need four coils, two in either hand, and to throw high and wide.

## Mooring lines on buoys with no pendant

For mooring buoys with no pendant you'll need to attach a proper mooring line, or preferably two for safety, if you're staying any length of time. If you are staying just for lunch you can probably hang off your lasso. The line will chafe but not so that it will part, I wouldn't think. It does depend on the sea state and the movement of the boat. If there is a lot of movement you're probably not going to stop for lunch!

With your bow some distance from the water you will need to use a device to help you attach a proper mooring line to the buoy or you will have to deploy the dinghy.

Perhaps you could ask the harbourmaster to do it for you when he comes, because as sure as eggs is eggs he will be along shortly to collect his money. To retain control from on board I would make one end of the line fast on board, give the habourmaster the other end and ask him to take a turn round the shackle and hand the end back to you, which you can then secure on board. For safety, do the same with a second line. I expect this is what he would recommend.

## Be careful

Lassoing anything from the cockpit you need to be careful that you don't allow line to slip into the drink. Before deploying your lasso, or threading your bridle through the eye of the pendant, keep any line that comes from the bow on deck and inside the guard rails. And secure the end on a cleat. Once you have lassoed or threaded it, take up the slack and secure the line once more on the cleat. This is to ensure that there is no spare line in the water. Remember that thrusters can suck line into their tunnels just as props can wrap it around themselves, so keep the line clear of thrusters, too.

## The heavy-duty lasso

If there is any tide running though the moorings, an ordinary line will simply be flipped back off the buoy at you, so you will need to weight the lasso.

You create the heavy-duty lasso by taking a length of chain (about one metre) and slipping a length of heavy-duty plastic pipe over it. Then you can attach a line to both ends of the chain, which will give you a loop of line. This is useful because you don't have two ends to worry about – holding just one part of the line means you have both ends.

Or if you need the lasso to be very long then you could attach one rope to one end of the chain and another to the other end. Now you will have two ends and must make sure you retain both on board for success. You attach the ends exactly as you did for lassoing with a bridle.

I call this a lasso, but, unlike a normal rope lasso that you flick out and wide with your hands, the weighted lasso is so heavy that you can swing it only a little way from the side of the boat. So having got it over the buoy, you want it to catch on the chain below. Now

▲ Heavy-duty lasso.

▲ Here Rebecca is using an MOB strop (normally used to bring the casualty out horizontally, which is why it is covered in a 'safety orange' material). It makes a good heavy-duty lasso. The orange floating line forms a loop and Rebecca has tied another line to this. Note how she is showing Jonathan where the buoy is by positioning the lasso on the port bow.

▲ She drops the heavy-duty lasso over the mooring buoy.

▲ The boat drops back, and the line is attached to the boat. You can then haul yourself up to the buoy, attach a proper mooring line and remove the heavy-duty lasso.

allow the boat to drift off the buoy a little to give you that lateral element. And then haul in the line and bring the buoy to the bow.

## Overrunning the buoy

With a breeze from aft and a weak tide, it is quite possible that a motor cruiser will be blown into the mooring buoy by the wind. You can either lift the buoy so that it is out of the water or, better still, present the tide with as much resistance as possible. Full lock-on rudders or outdrives and trim tabs down fully are options. Trailing buckets off the stern is another.

You can also set the kedge anchor (see Chapter 9). You will have to use the dinghy to do this. Take the kedge anchor, chain and warp, dinghy off about 50 feet, drop the kedge anchor and chain, take the warp back to the boat and haul in until tight. The anchor is now set. Haul in further until your bow is no longer knocking against the mooring buoy.

# SLIPPING THE MOORING

## Pendant attached to a bow cleat

This can be dropped from the foredeck. If there is any tide running, the helm could click the engine into gear for a moment to allow some slack in the pendant so that the crew can remove it easily.

## Using a slipped line

To allow for a controlled departure, which can be managed from the cockpit, set up a slipped line. Assume that you have picked up the pendant of the buoy amidships on starboard and have threaded a bow bridle through it, the boat has been pushed downtide and the pendant is now by the bow. Take a line from a stern cleat along the starboard deck, thread it too through the eye of the pendant and then take it outside the stern head and the bow of the boat, then back on board and along the port deck, and secure it on a stern cleat on port.

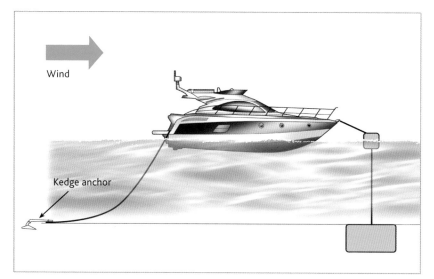

▲ Overrunning the mooring buoy? Set a kedge anchor.

Wind

Kedge anchor

▲ Slipped line set for controlled exit from the cockpit.

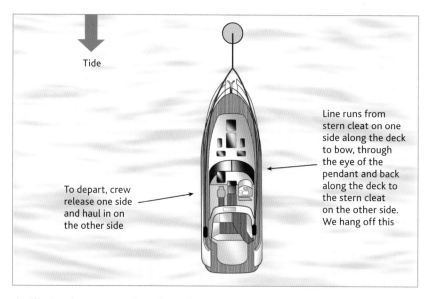

Tide

Line runs from stern cleat on one side along the deck to bow, through the eye of the pendant and back along the deck to the stern cleat on the other side. We hang off this

To depart, crew release one side and haul in on the other side

▲ Slipping the mooring – from the cockpit.

### TOP TIP

## Gelcoat protection

To protect your gelcoat from a rough pendant, thread a line through the eye of the pendant and attach this line to both port and starboard bow cleats to leave the pendant a little way clear of the boat.

Now release the bridle and the boat will hang off this new slipped line. To depart, take the line off one of the stern cleats and haul in on the line secured to the other stern cleat. All handled from the cockpit. The helm can tickle the engine in and out of gear to ensure you are not pushed downtide on to any boat astern of you if you are moored to one buoy in a line of moorings. The same applies if you are moored to a buoy with a ring, shackle or hoop: you need to set a line to slip.

Scan the QR code to watch a video of these techniques of how to pick up a mooring buoy:

# 9 ANCHORING

Lying safely to an anchor, over lunch or overnight, confident that you are holding, is a wonderful thing to do. And anchoring opens up new possibilities. You can stop the boat any time you like, you can anchor with others, you can anchor alone and enjoy those remote spots.

There really is only one thing that causes any difficulty with anchoring, and that is not paying out enough cable. And the reason that not enough cable is paid out is because the cable has not been coded. No one actually has any idea of how much chain is being veered. So the first thing you need to do is code the cable.

## CODING THE CABLE

You need a code that you can understand, that is immediately obvious, with markers that won't foul the gypsy when they go over it. Many people put a splodge of red paint every ten metres, but I cannot for the life of me remember, when I have returned suitably refreshed from the pub, how many splodges of paint I have let out. Paint also flakes off over time. In any event, I think that marking the chain in five-metre intervals is more useful. I often anchor in three or four metres of water. So you need a code.

▲ You rarely see a motorboat displaying an anchor ball. Here's a rare example.

▲ Splodges of paint. What does that really tell you?

# Snooker

For some reason I seem to be able to remember the order in which you pot the snooker balls, despite not playing the game.

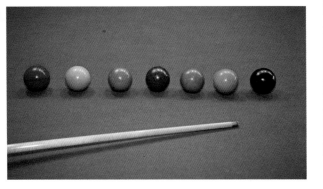

▲ Coding the anchor.

And so I mark my chain with silks tied in at five-metre intervals in the order that snooker balls are potted: red, yellow, green, brown, blue, pink, black. And because that gets me to only 35 metres and my chain is 50 metres in length, I go back to the beginning and double up:

| | | |
|---|---|---|
| 1 × red | = | 5m |
| 1 × yellow | = | 10m |
| 1 × green | = | 15m |
| 1 × brown | = | 20m |
| 1 × blue | = | 25m |
| 1 × pink | = | 30m |
| 1 × black | = | 35m |
| 2 × red | = | 40m |
| 2 × yellow | = | 45m |

▲ All chain with silks tied to the links.

▶ Chain and warp with silks tied into the octoplait warp.

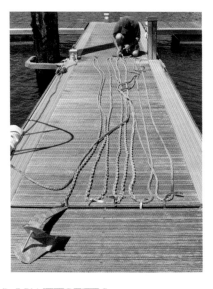

Place the anchor on the dock and pull out all the chain from the anchor locker and with a tape, measure off the five-metre intervals.

Now if I see a piece of blue silk flying above the water I know I have 25 metres of cable out.

▶ Blue: snooker code for 25 metres.

If snooker means nothing to you then you can run the colours alphabetically:

| | | | |
|---|---|---|---|
| 1 × black | = | 5m |
| 1 × blue | = | 10m |
| 1 × brown | = | 15m |
| 1 × green | = | 20m |
| 1 × pink | = | 25m |
| 1 × red | = | 30m |
| 1 × yellow | = | 35m |
| 2 × black | = | 40m |
| 2 × blue | = | 45m |

If the cable is mainly rope (or warp as it's called) you will have ten metres of chain between the anchor and the warp, to help the anchor dig in and set. You can tie the silks into the strands, whether it's three-strand or multiplait, or you can bind coloured cotton around.

It is also important to put this code inside a foredeck locker lid so that new crew know what it all means.

You can use any system, but the ones I mention make sense. And, of course, the alphabetical system works in any language. I gave a talk to a Welsh yacht club and I thought I'd endear myself to them by showing them how the code would go alphabetically in Welsh.

It went down a treat. Turns out that 11% of Welsh people use spoken Welsh quite regularly and several of the audience very much liked the idea of having their anchor cable coded according to the Welsh alphabet.

## Welsh code

| | | | |
|---|---|---|---|
| 5m | = | Coch | ▬ |
| 10m | = | Du | ▬ |
| 15m | = | Glas | ▬ |
| 20m | = | Glyrdd | ▬ |
| 25m | = | Gwrm | ▬ |
| 30m | = | Melyn | ▬ |
| 35m | = | Pinc | ▬ |
| 40m | = | 2 × Coch | ▬ |
| 45m | = | 2 × Du | ▬ |

Now with a system like this you know precisely how much cable you have veered. And knowing that you have veered the correct amount of cable is the secret to stress-free anchoring.

I call these silks **Anchor Buddie,** and you can order them at: westviewsailing.co.uk/anchor-buddies/. The silks are mounted on a laminated card, which has the five essentials of anchoring on the reverse as a reminder, and there is a separate laminated card with the code, which goes on the inside of the foredeck locker lid. You can choose either the snooker code or the alphabet code.

Do the silks last long? The image below shows what they looked like after three years of anchoring and being kept in the filthy anchor locker along with the rusty chain.

▲ Silks and cotton round warp.

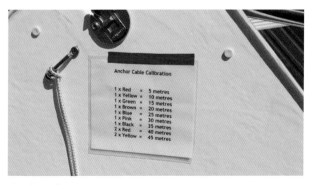

▲ The code.

▲ Silks after three years of constant use.

# ANCHORING ESSENTIALS

So now you have your cable coded, you can set about anchoring and the first thing you need to do is to go through the five essentials of anchoring.

# GROUND TACKLE

You also need ground tackle that is man enough for the job – an anchor and chain or a chain/rope combination that are the correct specification for the boat.

You see the full range of anchors when you look round a marina, but the most popular on motorboats will be the Delta and the Bruce. You do see the occasional Rocna.

## Five essentials of anchoring

- **Shelter**
  Not a lee shore, or likely to become one, no nasty tides.

- **Not prohibited**
  Not a fairway, not a shipping lane, not restricted/prohibited.

- **Depth**
  Enough depth at low water and enough chain/warp at high water.

- **Holding**
  Will the bottom give good holding for your type of anchor? Mud and sand good, rock not always so good.

- **Swinging**
  Is there room to swing when the tide turns or if you are blown about by the breeze?

## Anchor options

| Type | Make | For | Against | Bottom |
|---|---|---|---|---|
| Fisherman | Fisherman | Folds flat. Good on rock and kelp | Poor power-to-weight ratio | Rock/kelp |
| Plough | CQR/Plough | Good all rounder. The hinged shank is designed to avoid tripping with the turn of the tide | The hinged shank doesn't always prevent it tripping with the turn of the tide, but it usually resets itself | All types, use a tripping line if anchoring on rock |
| | Delta | Strong, sets quickly, self launching | | All types, tripping line for rock |
| | Kobra | Strong, sets quickly, self launching | | All types, tripping line for rock |
| Claw | Bruce | Strong | | All types, tripping line for rock |
| Lightweight | Danforth (Steel) Fortress (Aluminium) Brittany | Stows flat. Can vary the angle of the flukes to match harder or softer seabeds | Can be hard to set in harder seabeds. Can trip and then not reset. Best used as a kedge anchor | Clay, sand and mud |
| Modern | Spade | Strong, sets quickly, self launching | | All types, tripping line for rock |
| | Rocna | Strong, sets very quickly, self launching | Check the quality of the steel, some were made with inferior steel | All types, tripping line for rock |
| | Manson Supreme | Strong, sets very quickly. Clever self-tripping slot, self launching | | All types, tripping line for rock |
| | Ultra | Strong, sets very quickly, self righting, self launching | | All types, tripping line for rock |
| Grapnel | Grapnel | Folds up, used for light work | Used as a kedge anchor or for dinghies | Anything really |

# GROUND TACKLE

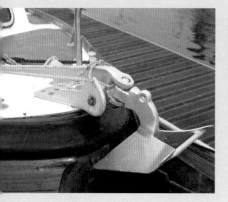

▲ CQR or plough secured with a lashing.

▲ Delta.

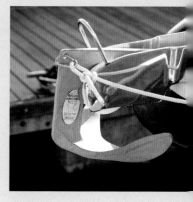

▲ Bruce secured on a lanyard.

▲ Rocna secured with a drop nose pin.

▲ Fortress is made from aluminium, while Danforth is made from steel.

▲ Ultra.

▲ Grapnel, with 10m chain, then warp.

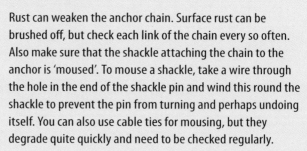

## Check the chain and mouse the shackle

Rust can weaken the anchor chain. Surface rust can be brushed off, but check each link of the chain every so often. Also make sure that the shackle attaching the chain to the anchor is 'moused'. To mouse a shackle, take a wire through the hole in the end of the shackle pin and wind this round the shackle to prevent the pin from turning and perhaps undoing itself. You can also use cable ties for mousing, but they degrade quite quickly and need to be checked regularly.

# HOW MUCH SCOPE TO ALLOW?

So assuming that your anchor will set in the seabed and hold you, you need to know how much cable to veer, or in English how much chain to pay out (the scope).

For peace of mind, the rule is a minimum of four times the depth for chain and a minimum of six times the depth for warp. When calculating depth don't forget to allow for the distance from the bow roller to the water, which can be anything from one metre on a 25ft boat to two metres on a 65ft boat. And if the wind is likely to pipe up, veer a little extra cable, assuming you have room in the anchorage. At the end of the day, as long as you have the room, chain in the anchor locker does no good at all, you might as well pay it out.

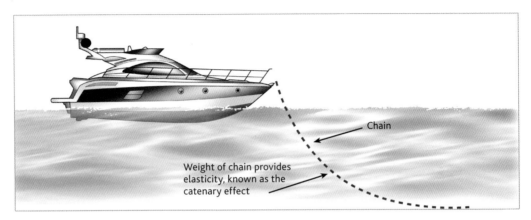

Chain

Weight of chain provides elasticity, known as the catenary effect

▶ Scope chain.

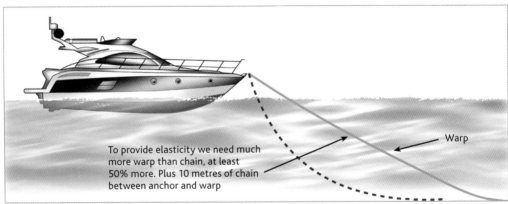

Warp

To provide elasticity we need much more warp than chain, at least 50% more. Plus 10 metres of chain between anchor and warp

▶ Scope warp.

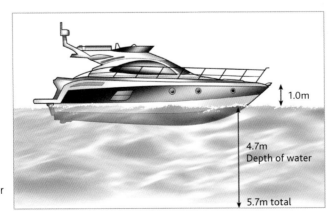

1.0m

4.7m
Depth of water

5.7m total

▶ Scope allowing for freeboard.

## How to calibrate the depth sounder

How do you know if your depth sounder is reading correctly?

To calibrate your depth sounder, you need a lead line (or a piece of cord with a weight attached would do it) and a tape measure. Measure on both sides of the boat. And do this as near to the transducer as possible. On *Hollywood* I was about ten feet abaft of it.

I always like to work to under keel or under prop rudder clearance. So that when the depth reads '0.00 the boat is aground. Some people like to work to depth of water, but then of course you must be very clear what your draught is when fully laden, with fub fuel and water tanks. It's up to you, but you need to know what your sounder is telling you, and your crew need to know this, too. Place a note by the depth sounder.

▲ Leadline and tape measure.

▲ Measuring on starboard.

▲ Measuring on port.

▲ Getting the reading.

◀ Four metres actual depth. What does the echo sounder say? Adjust it to read actual depth or depth below props and stern gear, whichever you prefer.

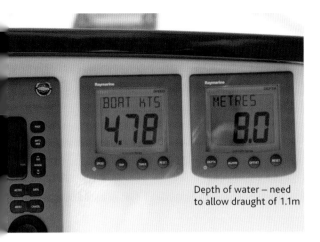

Depth of water – need to allow draught of 1.1m

▲ Depth of water.

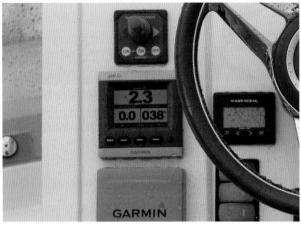

▲ Depth under prop.

## SOME QUICK TIPS FOR ANCHORING SUCCESS

### Setting the anchor

Always anchor into the tide, unless the strength of the wind is greater than the tide.

In tidal waters the pull of the boat as it is dragged back by the tide should get the anchor to set. In non-tidal waters, or at slack water, backing up to set the anchor will help.

### Snatching

If there is a bit of a chop and you find the boat is snatching at the anchor then veer more cable. Or you could add in a rope snubber tied to the chain with a rolling hitch (see Chapter 2) and then back on board to a cleat. Once secure, veer more chain so that the boat is holding to the snubber and chain, rather than the expensive windlass. In any event, always take the strain off the windlass by locking the chain off with a chain stopper (devil's claw) which you may have set into the deck or with a snubber.

### How to tell if your anchor is holding

The first way is to place your hand outside the bow roller on to the cable. If it is quiet you are holding. If it is vibrating you may be on the move.

▲ Chain lock.

▲ Hand-bearing compass. It's not vital for the purposes of establishing drag, but do check that any metal glasses do not deviate the compass!

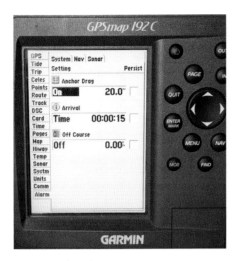

▲ GPS anchor alarm.

Fixing something on the shore and monitoring this by eye or bearing is another way, and setting your anchor watch on the GPS is yet another.

## Preventing the cable from jumping off the bow roller

If the anchorage is a bit lively, the boat is moving around a bit and you haven't set a snubber, there is always the chance that the anchor cable might jump off the bow roller. To stop this from happening add in a split pin or a lashing between the bow roller cheeks.

## Securing the anchor on board

You don't want the anchor jumping out of its moun and setting itself unexpectedly, so attach it to the boat A lashing will do, or a lanyard – often bow cheeks have a split pin for securing the anchor.

## Displaying the correct signal

The anchor signal by day is one black ball where it car best be seen in the 'forepart of the vessel'. At night you show an all-round white light where it can best be seen As most boats come with navigation lights, this does not present a problem. But how many people exhibit ar anchor ball by day? Gulets in the Mediterranean have a ball fixed permanently, which means they give exactly the correct signal when anchored and absolutely the wrong signal when under way.

But consider this: if you were in a charted anchorage during the day and you were exhibiting an anchor ball and someone were to run into you, then the fault and the responsibility would lie very clearly with the other party. If you were not exhibiting an anchor ball, however, they would be bound to claim that you were in contravention of the International Rules for the Prevention of Collisions at Sea and that it was you who was at fault, not them. Well, you would hope they wouldn't and that they would do the decent thing and

▲ Some bow cheeks have a hoop between the two to prevent the cable from jumping out.

▲ Here they used a lanyard and a split pin to hold the anchor in place.

admit liability, but where any insurance claim is in the offing, all bets are off. It's just a thought. You will notice that all the diagrams come with an anchor ball in place. Up by the radar arch is a good place to put it.

## Swinging room

When you approach an anchorage, look at how the other boats are lying. Heavy displacement sailing boats will lie to the tide rather than the wind. Flybridge motorboats with medium or deep V hulls will lie more to the wind than the tide. So if you are in an anchorage with a cross section of boats you need to keep well clear in case you get blown into them. If the anchorage is tidal, all boats will lie downtide to one degree or another and as the tide slackens so they will creep up to where their anchor has been set, as the weight of the chain will pull the boat forward. Then at slack water all the boats will mill around their anchor chains and then as the new tide kicks in they will turn and as the rate increases they will be set downtide again.

## What happens when the tide turns?

Anchors that bury themselves into the seabed will generally handle the turn of the tide without tripping. If they do trip you want them to set themselves again quickly. Danforths and Fortress anchors can be hard to

### Anchored or moored? **?**

- If you lie to one anchor you are anchored.
- If you lie to two anchors you are moored.
- If you lie to a mooring buoy you are moored.
- If you lie to a pile mooring, pontoon or finger berth you are moored.

### Lights when moored or anchored

You don't need to show an anchor light at night when moored to a buoy that is marked on the chart. Some people do, for added security, but it is not necessary.

reset and that is why they tend to be used as kedge anchors. The modern breed of Rocna and Manson anchors will reset themselves very quickly. Delta, Spade and CQR anchors should also reset themselves.

## Overrunning the anchor, being blown about by the wind?

As mentioned in Chapter 8, a breeze from aft and a weak tide can result in you being blown by the wind over the anchor cable. The wind may not be strong enough to be the dominant force, but until the tide sets in you may want to hold the boat back off the anchor. Or you may be blown about by the wind and spend time sailing about the anchor from one side to the other.

You need to present the tide with as much resistance as possible. Full lock-on rudders or outdrives and trim tabs down fully are options. Trailing buckets off the stern is another. Although that is a bit of a faff and it might be easier to set a kedge anchor.

### Rode or cable? **?**

Rode is American and refers to the rope (which, when used for anchoring or mooring, we call warp) or chain that attaches to the anchor. Cable is English for the warp or chain.

A cable is also a unit of measurement. The length of anchor warp on ships of the line was a cable or 100 fathoms or 600 feet, which equates to 182.88 metres. There being 1852 metres in a nautical mile, 182.88 is one tenth of a mile – well, close enough – and so one tenth of a mile is called a cable.

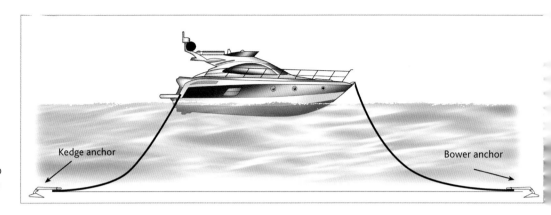

▶ Lying to a kedge anchor to hold you off the bower anchor.

Kedge anchor

Bower anchor

## Kedge anchor

A kedge anchor is a second anchor, the bower anchor (the anchor on the bow) being your primary anchor. The kedge anchor is so called because if you were, say, to run aground on a sandbank then you would row an anchor out in the dinghy, set it and then 'kedge' yourself off the sand bank. A kedge anchor can be any type of anchor, but they are often the Danforth or Fortress type.

To set the kedge anchor you drop the bower anchor first, then drive astern and pay out as much of the bower cable as possible. Then drop the kedge anchor, and while paying out the kedge anchor cable, haul in some of the chain on the bower anchor. Doing this should allow the kedge anchor to set. Make the kedge anchor cable fast on a stern cleat. Now you are lying to two anchors, one forward and one aft, and this will hold you in place.

You do need to weigh this anchor at slack water before the tide turns. If that happens to be in the middle of the night that is unfortunate. I always make sure I am awake for the turn of the tide if I am anchored, just to make sure that the anchor remains set after the turn.

## Anchor stuck?

If you can't get the anchor up because it is caught on something, try driving the boat over the anchor. Try working the boat around and lifting the anchor from different angles. If it really won't come up then you will need to leave the anchor (at least £750) and the chain (again at least £750) behind. As no one wants to lose £1500, it is worth buoying the chain, marking the spot with the MOB function on the GPS plotter and hoping that the local dive company will look kindly on you. On a good day, when they have other work in the area, the rate might be £500. On a bad day with a special call-out it might be £1000. You can't of course have just 'a diver', you will need a RIB, with a dive master, a diver and his buddy – three people.

### Tripping eye

You could, of course, attach a tripping line to the eyelet in the crown of the anchor, which will allow you to pull the anchor out backwards if it becomes stuck. To set this up in advance suggests that you're not confident of

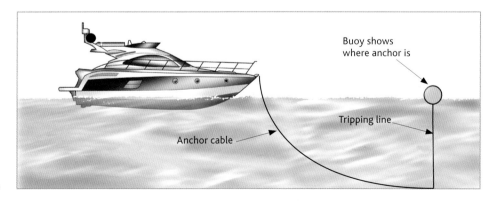

Buoy shows where anchor is

Tripping line

Anchor cable

▶ Tripping line and buoy set.

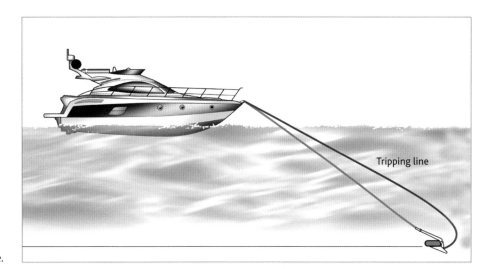

Tripping line

▶ Anchor caught under a cable.

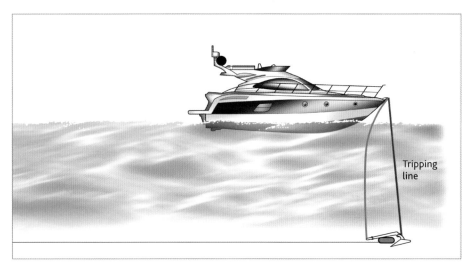

Tripping line

▶ Using a tripping line to free it.

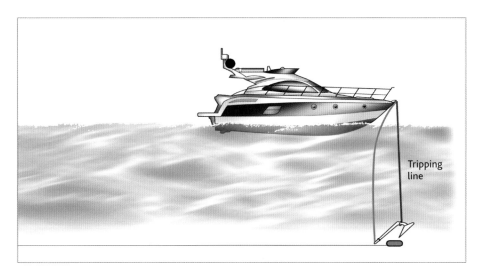

Tripping line

▶ Anchor free.

▲ Tripping line and buoy.

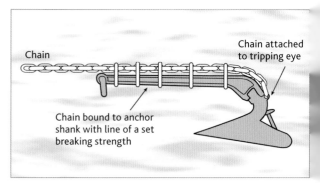

▲ Fisherman's trick 1.

▲ Attached to the tripping eye and ready to deploy.

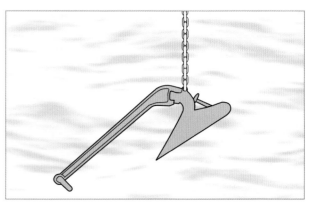

▲ Fisherman's trick 2.

the bottom, and if that was the case I would do my best to avoid anchoring there.

If I had to anchor in an emergency I might set a tripping line as a precaution. I already have an emergency, and I don't need another emergency when I find I can't get my anchor out. You can choose whether to keep the buoy of the tripping line on board or let it float to show others where your anchor is. It could be a useful guide to others to prevent them laying their anchor cable over yours.

Another option for retrieving an anchor that is stuck is to haul in the anchor cable until it is vertical. Take a sinking line, possibly weight it, tie a loose bowline around the anchor chain and allow this to drop to the bottom. The idea is to get this to go over the shaft of the anchor, which if lying horizontal it might do. Then haul on the line and lift the anchor out backwards.

Fishermen often attach the chain to the tripping eye of the anchor and then bind the chain to the shank with fishing line or indeed cable ties.

▲ This chap obviously fishes.

This way if the anchor does get stuck they simply drive over it, break the line or ties and now they are able to pull the anchor out backwards. This is fine for fishermen who are awake and at work when they are anchoring. I would not recommend this if you were to anchor overnight with the idea of having a peaceful night's sleep, just in case...

Many times people have told me that despite having the best anchor in the business they have trouble anchoring and that they always drag. And every time that has happened we have then coded the cable properly so they know how much they are letting out, we have calibrated the depth sounder so it reads correctly and we have confirmed that they will let out the right amount of chain for the depth they are in. And every time from that point on they have been able to anchor successfully whenever they chose.

▶ A gentleman's motor yacht lying quietly at anchor, an anchor ball showing where it can best be seen, in the 'forepart of the vessel'.

# 10 RIVERS AND CANALS

## CURRENT

Rivers flow from their source out to sea and therefore have a current that runs downstream. This increases enormously when it rains. Canals do not really have a current, but any lock that has just been emptied into a section of canal where you happen to be will send water in your direction and will produce a current. In fact, wherever you see white water expect an increase in current.

Current is strongest round the outside of the bend and weaker on the inside. Sometimes it will run round the outside, rebound off the bank and provide a back eddy on the inside bank, so there you might experience a slight upstream current.

And there will be less current in the shallows by the edge of a river.

Depth is likely to be greater on the outside of the bend as well, so do not take the racing line with 60 feet's worth of clank. Cutting the corner will very likely lead to disaster.

## BANK EFFECT

As you pass close to a riverbank you will see the water drawn by your propeller coming towards you between the boat and the bank and the water level will be lowered. This will draw your boat towards the bank. The natural reaction is to increase revs and try to steer away from it, but this simply magnifies the effect and you will be drawn to the bank even more. The answer is to put the engine into neutral and steer away from the bank. Then the boat will move away.

### Who gives way?

The downstream-bound boat is the stand-on vessel.

Upstream-bound vessels must give way.

This effect also occurs when boats pass each other, either when the other boat is coming towards you or when one of you is overtaking. This is why you need to give each other a bit of space, because if you are too close, you will be drawn towards each other.

The answer is to take the engine out of gear so you drift past each other. This will reduce the effect.

This 'bank effect' can be used in your favour. If you are about to move away from the bank or mooring and another boat goes past, its displacement of water will pull you off the mooring.

## GETTING ON AND OFF A PONTOON

Again, always moor into the current. It's what gives you your grip on the water and allows you to slow down.

### Single-handing a barge on a river

I have included this because it is a classic piece of boat handling and relates to all boats (be they barges, narrowboats, single-screw steel motorcruisers or twin-screw planing motorcruisers). Single-handing a barge uses the first principles of springs, prop walk, powering against lines and nice, relaxed seamanship.

The 56ft barge *Le Coq* is attached to the dock by a bow line and a breast line. Roy wants to spring the bow out into the current so he sets a slipped stern spring. He removes the bow line and the breast line, clicks the engine into astern and the bow comes away from the dock. With the engine in neutral, Roy retrieves the stern spring line. He puts the engine into ahead and moves off into the river.

He then turns the barge round. *Le Coq* kicks to starboard in astern, so a turn to port is favoured. Helm hard aport, a few revs astern to get the bow turning and then ahead to keep the turn going and the barge turns within its own length.

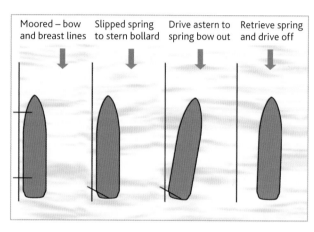

| Moored – bow and breast lines | Slipped spring to stern bollard | Drive astern to spring bow out | Retrieve spring and drive off |
|---|---|---|---|

▲ Springing out the bow.

▼ Barge *Le Coq.*

> **? Barge or narrowboat?**
>
> The difference between a barge and a narrowboat? It seems obvious to say, but one is narrower than the other.
>
> A narrowboat has a beam of no more than 7 feet. A barge has a beam of 14 feet plus.

# GETTING ON TO THE DOCK

▲ Roy slows the barge to a stop, leaves the wheelhouse and goes forward to lasso a pile.

▲ He then goes back to the wheelhouse and clicks the engine into ahead with some starboard rudder, so the barge drives against the bow line, and brings the stern into the dock.

▲ With the stern alongside, Roy lassoes a pile with the breast line: moored.

## Shortening a line

If the crew want to shorten a line to set it to slip and they will be holding on to it, then take a bight through a ring or around a pile. They will release the bight and haul in on the standing end when ready to depart.

Through a ring on a pile.

## How to tell the depth of water by the bank

Shallow water:

- Reeds growing (they need shallow water)
- Cattle drinking
- People swimming
- Bank falling into the river (this will reduce the depth)

Deeper water:

- Nice high bank, sheer-sided

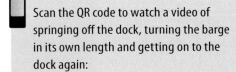

Scan the QR code to watch a video of springing off the dock, turning the barge in its own length and getting on to the dock again:

## HOW TO TIE A LINE ON TO A BOLLARD ON BOARD

Bollards have a spigot low down, which helps when trying to get a purchase on a line.

▲ O as if starting an OXO.

▲ Using the spigot…

▲ make the first half of the X.

▲ Then the second half of the X and a hitch.

## Communication lines

When the crew have released the line from the dock and the boat is free they should show the running end of the line to the helm. He may not be able to see what they are doing, especially if they are on a barge and some metres distant from him. This is a nice clear piece of communication, which applies to all boats.

**i**

If you are mooring at a waiting dock for a lock and you do not want to enter the lock at the time, cross your hands to tell the lock-keeper that you are not coming through.

Letting the lock-keeper know that you are not coming through.

## Lock

Approaching a lock and having to wait, Roy nudges the port side of the barge into the 'waiting dock', puts the engine into neutral, steps up to the bow and lassoes a palm head. Then, with the engine clicked into ahead and starboard helm to bring the stern in, he lassoes the breast line to a convenient bollard.

Mindful that passing boats would pull the barge away from the waiting dock, Roy releases the bow line just as the boats empty out of the lock. This pulls the barge away from the bank nicely. Roy releases the breast line and puts the barge into gear.

His technique in locks is to stop the barge, loop his breast line over a bollard on the lock side, and with this in hand walk forward and do the same with a bow line. Then, with the two lines in hand, he chats to the lock-keeper while the lock empties.

Note how everything has been done by lassoing and using slipped lines.

▲ Barge driving ahead against a bow line.

▶ Roy prepares to lasso the palm head on the dock to bring the stern in.

◀ Breast line led from bollard on barge round bollard on the lock side.

▼ Holding the barge on the two lines while the lock empties.

## Mooring by a riverbank single-handed

Roy chooses his spot and then from the middle of the river ferry glides to the bank. All the time he is measuring the rate of the current and the strength of the wind off the field and how the two of them are affecting the barge.

Yes, he does have 17 metres and 20 tons of unmanned barge driving against the bank for a short time.

To leave, Roy pulls out the breast spikes and places these and the breast line back on board. He then pulls out the spikes at the bow and steps back on board with the bow line. Back to the wheelhouse, a little

engine ahead with some port rudder gets the bow out into the stream and he is able to drive off.

This is a method endorsed by the RYA. It works for all boats, although any hull not made of steel might want to add in a bow fender. The key is that engines are just clicked into gear in tickover.

 Scan the QR code to watch a video of single-handed mooring to a riverbank:

# SINGLE-HANDED MOORING TO A RIVERBANK

▲ Roy drives the bow into the bank and balances the barge against the wind and current.

▲ He lashes the helm. A line the right length for this job might have been easier. This line is rather too long but it does the job.

▲ He then steps off the barge, drives a spike into the ground and takes a turn round it with the bow line.

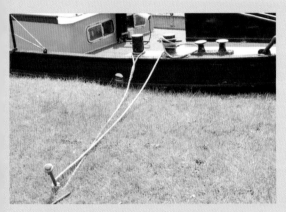

▲ Then it is back on board to release the lashed helm and turn it to port to bring the stern in.

▲ Ashore again, Roy drives in the spike for the breast line.

▲ He then drives a second spike across the first spike for the bow in a V to give them optimum holding power and OXOs the bow line to them.

▲ Then it is time for lunch…

▲ while the shorn sheep baa and fret about the mooring warps.

# TELL OTHER BOATS WHAT YOU ARE DOING

## Signals

The only one you need here is the anchor ball. Anchoring in a river is unusual, so you should let others know what you're doing by displaying an anchor ball. If it's not possible to mount it in the bow, hang it off the radar arch. Anywhere that it can be seen clearly.

## Sounds

I wouldn't worry about sound signals unless you are doing something unusual that others might not expect.

If you are on a narrowboat or a barge and you are turning right round in a river then you should let others know, and the sound signals are:

- Four short hoots, followed by one short hoot, when turning round to starboard

- Four short hoots, followed by two short hoots, when turning round to port.

If you are on the tidal stretch of any river and something big makes five very loud short hoots then it probably wants to know what your intentions are or for you to get out of the way.

The CEVNI regulations apply on inland waterways in Europe and you will need a certificate to say you have passed the CEVNI exam if you travel there. Bisham Abbey Sailing and Navigation School (www. bishamabbeysailing.co.uk) holds these courses, along with the regular RYA courses.

---

### ? Can you fit under the bridge?

It's a good idea to have a stick or mast on the bow that can bend, is tall enough for your air draught and beam and allows for the curvature of the bridge.

Here the top of the wind indicator is six inches above the coachroof.

Here the mast on the pulpit is just higher than the air draught with the flybridge lowered. It has been fixed loosely to allow it to move if it touches the roof of the bridge.

---

### i What a hoot

One short hoot: I am turning to starboard.

Two short hoots: I am turning to port.

Three short hoots: I am running my engines astern.

---

### TOP TIP Helm indicator

See where the helm is by having an indicator. Here *Le Coq* has a 'coq' with a green right eye and a red left eye. Nice and clear.

His other eye is red for port.

---

# COLREGS: IRPCS

These apply equally to rivers, although occasionally by-laws apply as well. The Port of London Authority has a rowing code of practice for the tideway, for example (www.pla.co.uk/assets/THE_ROWING_CODE.pdf). The Environmental Agency is responsible for regulating inland rivers in the UK.

And while motorboats give way to rowing boats, who give way to sailing boats, there could be an occasion in a shallow part of the river when a motorboat would be constrained by draught compared with a rowing eight, and then the rowing eight would have to give way to the motorboat. They would also have to keep out of the way until past and clear if they were overtaking.

## TOP TIP

### Bank security

Moored to a bank at night? Knock the pins in up to their eyes and padlock the eyes together to stop anyone lifting the pins. As you will have knocked the pins in at an angle to each other, they will have formed an upside-down 'V' under the ground. Now, with them locked together, it is impossible to lift them out.

At night cover the pins with a plastic bag, a bright plastic bottle or a yellow tennis ball so that walkers can see them.

## LOCK ETIQUETTE

**1.** If the lock is manned, do what the lock-keeper says.

**2.** Be careful not to place the bow or stern beyond any sign saying: 'Beware lock cill.' Getting caught on the cill is disappointing and expensive.

**3.** Never make fast a line. You'll be going up or down and need to keep your lines free to slip.

**4.** Lead the lines the right way under or over the guard wires for the lock you are in and for the direction of travel you will be encountering, up or down.

**5.** Lock-keepers do not like narrowboats using a centre line.

**6.** Keep fingers inboard.

▲ A pretty lock. Motorboats should always fender up well, especially in a lock.

▲ Ralph Tompkin, the lock-keeper at Boulter's Lock.

▲ The location of the lock cills will be indicated.

# 11 WEATHER

Weather is important to everybody. Sailors need wind but not too much of it. Motorboaters would rather there was no wind at all. There will be conditions that would make it no fun at all. It doesn't matter if you know nothing about the weather or if you are a budding Met Office forecaster, what follows will give you what you need or it may refresh what you already know. You see, when it comes to forecasting the weather for a small area, the area you will be sailing in, it is not very difficult.

In the UK, if you tell me we have low pressure I will tell you that the wind will be from the south, south-west very likely, and it could be quite strong. It will be overcast, the air will generally be warmer and rain will be in the offing. If you tell me we have high pressure then the wind will be from the north, it will be lighter, the sky will be clear, the air will be colder and there will very likely be no rain.

So from a very general statement, 'we have low pressure/we have high pressure', you can forecast quite specifically. Of course, you need a bit more information to be able to forecast accurately. But this high pressure/low pressure business will be the same the world over. With low pressure you will get certain weather and with high pressure you will get another type of weather.

Pressure differences are all about temperature and temperature is all about the sun. The sun heats the earth up, the air above the surface warms and rises. Where that air rises, lifting a weight off the earth, the pressure will be low. As the air rises through the atmosphere it cools and water vapour in the air condenses out as cloud. If the air continues to cool it will reach a point where it will form droplets of water and these will fall out of the cloud as rain.

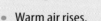

## Some general rules

- Warm air rises.
- Warm air rising takes weight off the ground and therefore reduces the pressure.
- Cold air falls.
- Cold air falling adds weight to the ground and increases the pressure.
- Warm air holds more water than cold air.
- Warm air cools as it rises.
- When it cools to a certain degree the water vapour in the air condenses out as cloud.
- When it cools even further this water vapour condenses out as droplets of rain or ice. The temperature at this point is called the dew point.
- Cold air moves faster than warm air.
- Wind wants to blow from high pressure to low pressure but is deflected by the Coriolis force and by friction from the ground so the wind blows more or less parallel to the isobars (lines of equal pressure) – at right angles to the pressure gradient, which is why the wind is referred to as the gradient wind.
- Wind direction is always described as where it is blowing **from**. So a north wind is blowing from the north.

So weather is all about differences in the temperature of air. As one parcel of air rises, reducing pressure, another parcel of air falls, increasing pressure. That's why weather is measured in differences in pressure.

► The passage of a depression.

▼ Match the letters on this synoptic chart to those on the diagram on the right showing the passage of a low to see what you can expect at each stage.

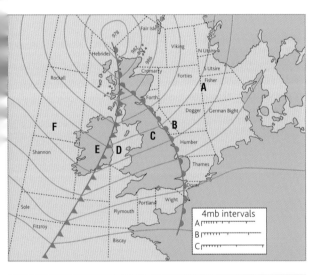

| | F | E | D | C | B | A |
|---|---|---|---|---|---|---|
| Wind | ↘ | ↘ | → | → | ↗ | ↗ |
| Wind | Strong gusts | Veers sharply, squalls | Steady | Veers | | Backs and increases |
| Pressure | Rises, then stable | Rises quickly | Steady | Steady | | Falls |
| Rain | Sunny, squally showers | Heavy rain, thunder, hail | Light rain | Drizzle | | Becomes heavier |
| Visibility | Good except in showers | Poor in rain | Poor, fog | Poor | Poorer | |
| Temp | Cold | Falls | Warm | Warm | Rising | |

4mb intervals

## WEATHER SCENARIOS

### Sunny day

This is a result of cold air falling, high pressure. Cold air falling, the skies are clear and the sun is able to warm up the ground and you have a warm sunny day. At night it will cool quickly and you will notice the coolness of the cold air falling.

### Cloudy, rainy day

This is a result of warm moist air rising, low pressure. Warm moist air rises and cools. The vapour condenses out as cloud. If it cools further this cloud reaches the dew

▲ Sunny day, cold air falling.

▲ Warm air rising and condensing out as cloud and rain.

point and droplets of rain are formed, or perhaps ice. At night, with it being overcast, the ground is unable to radiate its heat as it would if the sky had been clear, and you have warm air rising so the night air is not so cold.

## Cloud on a sunny day

The sun has warmed the ground, a parcel of warm moist air has risen and cooled and condensed out as cloud.

# WHAT THE CLOUDS MEAN

## Cirrus cloud

The highest level of cloud that has been beaten up by a great deal of wind and is wispy. The wispy effect is the ice crystals (it is very high in the sky and therefore very cold up there) that have been blown to smithereens by this strong wind. Cirrus invariably tells you that a depression is on the way.

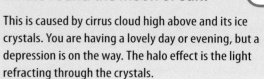

### A halo round the moon or sun?

This is caused by cirrus cloud high above and its ice crystals. You are having a lovely day or evening, but a depression is on the way. The halo effect is the light refracting through the crystals.

## Cumulus cloud

What do you call a sheep with no legs? A cloud. This is a description of the fluffy cumulus cloud which is caused by the sun warming up the ground, and the air above it rising (warm air rises) and then, as it rises, cooling. The water vapour in the air then condenses out as cloud, cumulus cloud. A cumulus cloud is associated with high pressure, cold air falling, cold air that has been warmed as a result of the sun beating down on the earth, which has caused this cold air to warm up and rise and the vapour within it to condense out as cumulus cloud.

## Stratus

Stratus means layered. Cirrus clouds are individual and distinct, cumulus clouds are separate, while stratus is general – a covering or layer.

## Nimbus

Means rainy. A nimbus cloud will be grey and contains rain. You will need an umbrella if you stand under a nimbus cloud. Nimbus is often general and layered and is referred to as nimbostratus. Nimbus clouds will be associated with low pressure, and with warm air rising and condensing out as cloud and then, when the dew point is reached, as rain.

## Cumulonimbus

This is the storm cloud that you find before a cold front. It is a system of its very own, with warm air rising up inside and cold air falling down at the sides. Aeroplanes will want to avoid this type of cloud as the updraft and downdraft can rip wings off. A cumulonimbus cloud will bring thunder and lightning.

## Lapse rate

The rate at which air cools as it rises is called the adiabatic lapse rate. Dry air cools 10°C every 1000 metres it rises. Moist or saturated air cools at the rate of 5.5°C every 1000 metres it rises.

Dry air is air that contains its moisture content invisibly.

Saturated air is air where the moisture content has condensed out as fog or rain.

## Why do winds blow…

anticlockwise round a low in the northern hemisphere and clockwise in the southern hemisphere? Because of the Coriolis force.

Scan this QR code to see a graphic description of the Coriolis force in action:

# FRONTAL SYSTEMS

A low-pressure system (cyclone/depression) has warm air rising and winds rushing into it, converging.

A high-pressure system (anti-cyclone) has cold air falling and winds rushing out of it, diverging.

The key to forecasting the weather is to look at the synoptic charts and the sky and to monitor the pressure. And to keep doing this until you can match what you are seeing with what the charts are telling you.

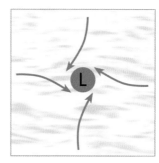

▲ A low: warm air rising, winds converge.

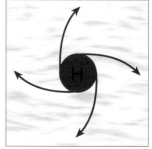

▲ A high: cold air falling, winds diverge.

## Isobars

• Close together: windy and rainy

• Further apart: less wind, sunshine

Even during the passage of a depression there will be areas where there will be sunshine and less wind – just look for a widening of the isobars.

I enjoy weather a great deal, and knowing a little about it gives you a different aspect. Where friends might say, 'Blast, it is raining again,' I will say, 'Ah, just as I expected. I am quite pleased because I thought it would be raining just now.' A little understanding gives you a little ownership of the subject.

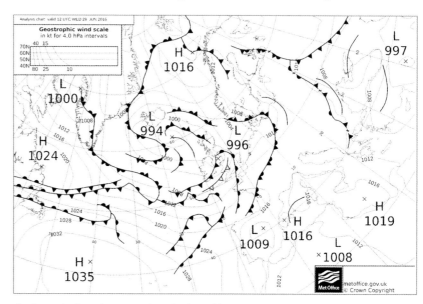

▲ Synoptic chart showing isobars, highs and lows.
[*Contains public sector information licensed under the Open Government Licence v1.0*]

# THINGS THAT AFFECT YOU

## Buys Ballot's law

With the wind to your back the low will be on your left (in the northern hemisphere), and the high will therefore be to your right. In the southern hemisphere this is reversed.

## Wind direction and fronts (northern hemisphere)

- *Warm front:* Wind backs before the front and then veers as it goes through and strengthens.
- *Mid front:* Wind direction stays steady.
- *Cold front:* As the front goes through, the wind veers sharply.
- *Occluded fronts:* Wind veers as the front goes through.

## Wind, land and sea

- Wind backs as a result of friction by 15° when it blows over sea.
- Wind backs as a result of friction by 30° when it blows over land.

## Converging and diverging wind

Wind blowing parallel to a coastline where the sea is to the left of the land will be stronger (the wind on the land is backed by 30° and the wind over the sea is backed by 15° so they are converging).

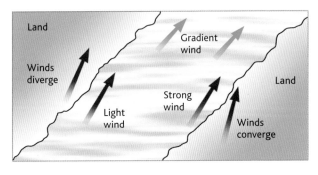

▲ Converging and diverging winds.

Wind blowing parallel to a coastline where the sea is to the right of the land will be weaker (the wind on the sea is backed by 15° and the wind on the land is backed by 30° so the two are diverging).

This is worth bearing in mind when you're crossing the Channel. With a south-westerly wind, the wind near the French coast will be stronger than the predicted gradient wind. Wind near the English coast will be weaker than the predicted gradient wind.

## Sea breeze

Land heats up and cools down quicker than water. The sun beating down on the water and land by the coast will heat the land up without affecting the temperature of the water. This temperature difference is what causes a sea breeze. The land heats the air above it, which rises and expands. This rising air causes the pressure a few hundred feet above the land to become greater than at the same height over the sea, a sort of vertical pile-up of air at height.

And so a flow begins at height, from overland to oversea. The air near the surface on the land is depleted, so pressure there falls. At the same time, for a similar column of air over the sea the pressure remains comparatively high. And as wind wants to blow from high pressure to low pressure, there is a flow near the surface from sea to land: a sea breeze. This carries on until the heat source stops, the sun sets.

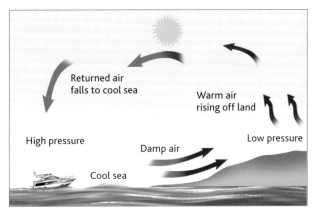

▲ Sea breeze. The sun warms the ground. The air above is warmed and rises. As it cools, the water vapour inside condenses out as cloud.

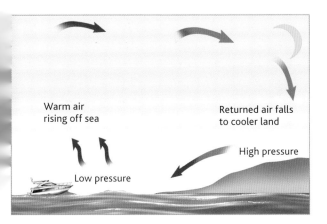

▲ Land breeze.

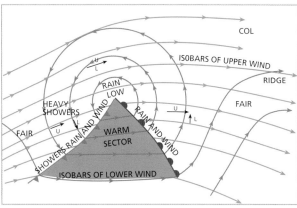

▲ Crossed winds rule.

## Land breeze

When the sun sets the land cools quickly, to the point that the sea is warmer than the land and the process starts again, only in reverse. Air warmed by the sea rises and expands, heads inland at height and a wind blows from the higher pressure on the land to the lower pressure over the sea: a land breeze.

## Crossed winds rule

If you stand with your back to the wind and the upper wind, or rather the clouds, move across you from left to right, then the weather will deteriorate. You are in front of the depression.

If you stand with your back to the wind and the upper wind or clouds come from right to left, the weather will improve. You are at the back of or behind the low.

Worth knowing. You can apply this to what you are experiencing in terms of pressure, wind strength and weather.

In front of a warm front (clouds moving across you from left to right), the pressure will have dropped, it will be raining and the wind will have increased in strength.

At the cold front (clouds moving across you from right to left), the pressure will be rising, and there will be squally showers but also gaps of blue in the sky as the weather is improving.

In the southern hemisphere the crossed winds rule applies when you are facing the wind, wind blows in a clockwise direction around a low and Buys Ballot's law is opposite that of the northern hemisphere.

You also need to consider wind and tide and how this affects you as you traverse the water.

## HOW WIND AFFECTS THE WATER

When the wind blows over the water it piles the water up into wavelets and then waves. And the greater the distance of the stretch of water (the fetch) that the wind is able to blow over, the bigger the waves. Added to which, if at the same time the seabed is shelving and the depth of water is reducing (which encourages the waves to break, as it does on a beach), then the wind blowing over this will have an even greater effect and will pile the waves higher. The Bay of Biscay is an

▲ Direction of wind according to wavelets.

example of this. The wind has come thousands of miles, the seabed shelves and there are generally significant waves to be found in Biscay.

On a calm day you can tell where the puffs of wind are because you see a darkened patch of water where the wind has made little wavelets. The direction of the wind is always at 90° to the line of the wavelets.

## Wind over tide

If the wind blows in the opposite direction to that of the tide (that is to say, a wind from the north is blowing over a tide which is setting to the north), then the wind will make wavelets and then waves, and these will be short and steep. They will make for an uncomfortable ride whether you drive into them or across them or go with them. This is referred to as 'wind over tide'.

However, if the wind is blowing in the same direction as the set of the tide, the wind will flatten out the water and provide you with a comfortable ride whichever direction you are travelling in – with the tide, against it or across it. It's worth driving into a 2-knot tide in this case, even if your 35-knot boat speed will actually deliver only 33 knots over the ground as you are being set back by the tide, because at least you would have a comfortable ride.

## Wind speed

### True wind
This is the wind that you experience when you are standing still on land.

### Apparent wind
The minute you start to move, you experience apparent wind. If there is no wind and the tide is slack and I start to motor at 10 knots at 360° (north), I will experience an apparent wind of 10 knots on the bow. The apparent wind speed is 10 knots and the apparent wind direction is north.

If, however, there is a true wind from the north of 10 knots and I decide to motor north at 10 knots, my apparent wind speed will be the 10 knots I am making over the ground plus the 10 knots from the gradient wind from the north: 20 knots.

If I were to drive south at 10 knots while the wind was blowing from the north at 10 knots, I would experience an apparent wind speed of zero as the two would cancel each other out – my forward speed of 10 knots and the following wind of 10 knots – and the apparent wind direction would be impossible to define as there would be no wind.

True and apparent wind speed are not so important to a motorboat because when you are planing at 30 knots, even if there is no gradient wind, you are experiencing a wind speed of 30 knots, which is Force 7 – a near gale. If you increase speed to 35 knots you are creating your very own gale – Force 8.

## MOON PHASES

Knowing the state of the tide just by looking at the phase of the moon is very handy indeed. When you see a D shape in the sky the moon is waxing, going from a new moon to a full moon (both spring tides). A perfect D indicates a neap tide, more or less.

When you see a C shape the moon is waning. And no matter where in the world you are, high water springs at your home port will be at the same time, +/- 1 hour, every time, while high water neaps will be about six hours different, +/- 1 hour, every time. In Southampton, HW springs is, roughly speaking, at 1200 and 0000, with neaps at 0600 and 1800. In Plymouth HW springs is roughly 0700 and 1900, with neaps at 0100 and 1300.

Tides advance roughly 50 minutes in every 24 hours. So high water this morning at 1000 means high water tomorrow morning will be at 1050. Without looking at a tide table, if I see a full moon I know HW Southampton is roughly 1200, so high water three days hence, say, will be roughly at 1430 (3 x 50 = 150min, which is 2h 30min on from 1200). High water in seven day's time will, of course, be neaps, so six hours different from springs: 0600 and 1800 for Southampton.

So when I am at home and I see a full moon I know the time of high water at my marina, and if I see a crescent moon I know what the time of high water will be. Anything in between and I will have to make an educated guess and, of course, I always confirm my estimate with the almanac.

I also know that the pressure is higher rather than lower (clear sky as opposed to overcast), and that tells me that the wind will be more northerly. Overcast, a low, will give more southerly winds. So I have a great deal of information before I even set off from home, just by looking at the sky.

If you're a Solent sailor and you want to take advantage of the tides and save some money, you can add in the fact that the tide in the Solent turns an hour before HW Portsmouth and that means the tide will be flowing to the west. So opting to head east in the

## Stars and planets

Stars twinkle, planets don't. That's not strictly true but near enough. Stars and planets, even the sun and the moon, all twinkle to some degree. As their light reaches earth it passes through air, and turbulence in the earth's atmosphere causes the light to refract differently from one moment to the next. To us the object is seen to jigger about or twinkle or, as the astronomers say, 'scintillate'. The further away an object, the greater the effect. Stars are much, much, much further away than planets and the sun and the moon, so they are more likely to appear to 'scintillate'.

Solent into the ebbing tide will cost you much more than if you headed west with the ebbing tide. Your best bet is to head west, Yarmouth say, have a long lunch at Salty's, followed by some afternoon tea, and head back on the flooding tide from 5 o'clock onwards.

# 12 NAVIGATION

▲ Corbière Lighthouse, Jersey: best passed one mile off.

## SPEED LIMITS

Speed limits are set by harbour and river authorities to try to reduce wash in order to preserve the banks and to provide a comfortable environment for other boaters who may be moored on buoys or in marinas or, indeed, for rowing boats. All speed limits are maxima and if you are making a great deal of wash at four knots in a six-knot speed limit, slow down until you are making little or no wash. This is not easy if you have a pair of 1000hp Mann diesels on your boat. Clicking one engine into gear on slow idle may be enough to take you past the six-knot limit.

And here's a point: the six-knot limit refers to speed through the water, not speed over the ground, but many boaters are measuring their speed from the chart plotter or GPS, which will be giving them speed over ground.

If there is a two-knot tide or stream and you are going with it, and the GPS says you are doing six knots, you are actually going only four knots through the water. The other two knots of speed are courtesy of the tide or stream. And if you are going against a two-knot tide, six knots on the GPS will actually mean that you are going eight knots through the water. This is likely to mean that you are creating too much wash.

▲ Speed limit sign.

Of course, hull shape makes an enormous difference and some motorboats can slip along quite happily at six knots with very little wash. Indeed, slipper boats, so called because the first of these designs (built for Lady Astor) had a stern that resembled a slipper, when driven at a sensible cruising speed create practically no wash at all.

You're still not supposed to go more than six knots through the water, even if you make no wash at all. Because speed limits are set not just to protect the environment from damage but also in relation to what is appropriate for the traffic density. Going at eight or nine knots in a narrow river doesn't give anyone else much of a chance and is too fast for the confined waters.

And you really can help yourself and others if you pay attention to the wash you are creating and keep it to a minimum.

On the Thames at Richmond the default setting for all oarsmen when they spot a motorboat approaching is a scowl. They lay down their oars ready to shout and gesticulate as they are bounced around and swamped by the wash. They have a freeboard of only a few inches. And it is so unnecessary. Much better to slow right down, create no wash and get a reluctant but cheery enough smile and wave from the oarsmen. Rowers are just so accustomed to being run down by motorboats and swamped that they automatically assume the worst. See Chapter 10 for who gives way to whom.

A good piece of advice is to clean the impeller of your log, which gives you speed through the water, and

calibrate it so you can read true boat speed, but it is unlikely to be widely accepted. And so most people will be reading speed from the GPS. To make sure you are abiding by the rules you should be aware of the tide or stream and concentrate on ensuring that your wash is kept to a minimum when in confined waters.

## GPS AND PAPER CHARTS

GPS is the most brilliant thing ever and as you get a digital read-out of your position to within two metres, 24 hours a day, 365 days a year, I would use it! And you do. But you must remember that it can go wrong. We rely on GPS throughout life. If the satnav in the car packs up then we will be lost. If the GPS on the boat packs up we will also be lost. But being lost on the road is a lot safer than being 'lost at sea'. So it makes sense to have a back-up. Much as you might have a map in the car, you need to have navigational charts so you can find your way.

Get used to referring to the charts each time you go out. If you haven't already, take an RYA Day Skipper course. You will find, if your GPS goes on the blink, that there are several other ways of getting your position:

- Visually: are you beside a known mark, a buoy that you can locate on your paper chart?

- Your DSC radio may have GPS on board and will give you your latitude and longitude.

- You can download apps on to your phone that will give you lat and long.

- GPS phones can tell you where you are. Some of these work by receiving the Navstar satellite signal and are true GPS, while others use triangulation from mobile phone masts.

Of course, if the GPS signal in your area has gone down then no other true GPS-based device will be able to receive the signal. If you are within range of mobile phone masts then your mobile phone should be able to give you a position. Failing that, you will need to rely on traditional methods: three-point fix, single-point fix and depth, transit and cross bearing etc.

## Fog

If you get caught out in fog – and it's easy to do as the fog rolls in very quickly – head for shallower water. If the GPS packs up at this point you will need to follow the paper chart. As long as you have calibrated your depth sounder and know what it is reading (depth of water or under keel/under prop clearance) and you know what the height of tide at that moment is, then you can follow a depth contour to get to a safe harbour. Depth of water is made up of height of tide and chart datum. Practise motoring down a depth contour to see how you would do it if you had to.

The other option in fog is to anchor and wait.

Do make sure your depth sounder is calibrated (see Chapter 9).

## Markers and buoys

It is easy to come unstuck in pilotage in confined waters when going from one buoy to the next. If a mark is missed it can mean that a corner is cut and then a grounding may result. You need to look at the chart, the chartlet in the almanac etc. before setting off. You really must leave a port-hand marker to port when entering a harbour and a starboard-hand marker to starboard. It is reversed as you exit the harbour, of course. If you do find that the mark you are looking at is not the one you expected, stop and do not move on until you have found out where you are and where you need to go next.

A safe water mark or fairway buoy will have water on either side of it so you can pass it on either side, but by convention you leave it to port so that you will always be travelling down the right-hand side of the fairway.

### Cardinals

Know your buoys. Cardinals tell you where the safe water is.

Some cardinals also have a Racon, a radar beacon that is activated by the sweep of your radar beam and sends back a Morse signal which appears on your radar. Handy in fog.

▲ Safe water mark, also called a fairway buoy.

▲ Here is a west cardinal: safe water to the west.

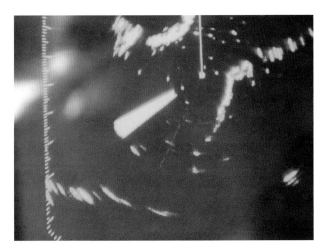
▲ Here the letter 'T', in Morse code 'dah', is splashed down the left-hand side of the radar from a Racon.

▲ Dennis the Menace: isolated danger mark.

▲ Here is a special mark: a racing buoy.

▲ Emergency wreck marking buoy.

## Isolated danger marks

Isolated danger marks have two black balls, post colour black with one or more red bands: Dennis the Menace's T-shirt is red and black. You would want to keep away from Dennis the Menace, so keep away from an isolated danger mark. The light will be two white flashes during the sequence, which might be five or ten seconds.

## Other marks

Special marks are yellow and have an X on the top.

Emergency wreck marking buoys are blue and yellow.

**TOP TIP**

### Avoiding pots at night

Avoid the lobster and crab pots and their markers by going down inside narrow channels and precautionary areas at night, as these will not have any pots laid in them. Go outside and you will encounter pots. Be aware of other traffic that has priority in the narrow channel or area and move outside to keep out of their way, if there is anyone coming.

## Lights

On a chart all lights will be white unless the colour is stated. In the past a light was indicated by a magenta teardrop. Now they are shown with a teardrop that matches the colour of the light, except that white lights have a yellow teardrop, the same as yellow lights. The symbol for the colour of the light will always be written as well: R, G, Y, W.

You need to know the difference between flashing, occulting and isophase. It's also useful to know the Morse code for 'U' and 'A' as they are often used as light rhythms, especially on safe water marks.

## Course to steer

Is there any point? Well, it depends on your speed – the slower you go, the greater the effect of the tide on your boat.

At seven knots a cross tide of two knots represents 29% of your boat speed. At 30 knots, two knots is just under 7% of your boat speed. The simple fact is that if you don't account for the tide, whether you are going at 7 or 30 knots, after one hour you will still end up two miles downtide of your destination.

If you are in confined waters in daylight you don't really worry about allowing for a cross tide. You can see it and use charted marks and landmarks to guide you. If you are crossing the English Channel and are out of sight of land, however, a course to steer is a good idea.

You can put a waypoint into the chart plotter and can stay on this line (bearing) to your destination by adjusting the helm or autopilot until your Course Over Ground line matches up with it. Without having to work anything out, you will now be running along a course to steer.

But if the GPS stops working, you might want to have a back-up plan. You can do a course to steer in your head.

 Scan the QR code to watch an amusing video on course to steer:

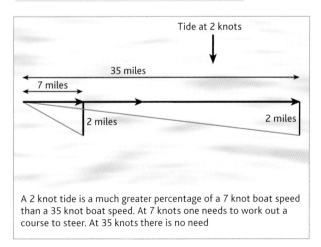

A 2 knot tide is a much greater percentage of a 7 knot boat speed than a 35 knot boat speed. At 7 knots one needs to work out a course to steer. At 35 knots there is no need

▲ Course to steer.

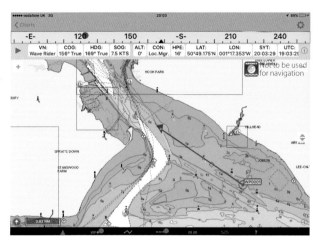

▲ The blue line is the bearing line. The yellow line is the predicted Course Over Ground. The boat is well off course.

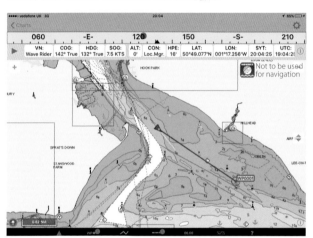

▲ By turning to port you can make the yellow line…

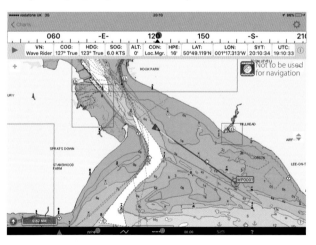

▲ follow the blue line. On course now.

First establish which hour of the tide you will be sailing in and the tidal set and rate for the bit of sea you will be travelling across. If you need help here, then an RYA course might be the answer or a visit to www.westviewsailing.co.uk and the video tutorials. You need three videos, 'The Tidal Hour', 'Tidal Diamonds & the Tidal Stream Atlas' and 'Course To Steer', to get the idea of the concept and to know where to find the information.

Then when you know the set (direction of the tide) and the rate (the speed), you can do a course to steer in your head.

## EXAMPLE CALCULATION OF A COURSE TO STEER

Let's say your destination lies due east of us: 090°. Your speed through the water (boat speed) is 12 knots.

The set of the tide is 180° so it is on your beam, pushing you south of your destination at a rate of two knots. So at the end of one hour you would be two miles south of your destination if you simply steered 090°.

▶ See Diagram 1.

To counter the effect of the tide and arrive exactly at your destination, use this simple formula.

60 x the speed of the tide in knots ÷ your boat speed in knots = the degree to which you need to counter the effect of the tide to stay on track for your destination.

So here this will be:

60 x 2 knots = 120 ÷ 12 knots = 10°.

So if you steer 10° into the tide you will go straight down the 090° line to your destination.

Your course to steer is 090° − 010° = 080°.

You will be going down your 090° bearing line, but you will be crabbing down it as you will point (the heading of the boat) in the direction of 080°.

▶ See Diagram 2.

If the tide is not exactly on the beam but on the shoulder or the quarter and if you wanted to be very accurate you would take a percentage of its effect. You would use just 70% of it.

So 10° was the course alteration when the tide was beam on, and when on the shoulder or quarter you would use 70% of 10° = 7°. You would steer 090° - 007° = 083° to remain on track.

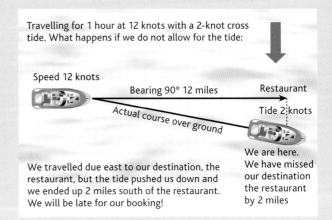

Travelling for 1 hour at 12 knots with a 2-knot cross tide. What happens if we do not allow for the tide:

Speed 12 knots

Bearing 90° 12 miles — Restaurant

Actual course over ground

Tide 2 knots

We are here. We have missed our destination the restaurant by 2 miles

We travelled due east to our destination, the restaurant, but the tide pushed us down and we ended up 2 miles south of the restaurant. We will be late for our booking!

▲ Diagram 1.

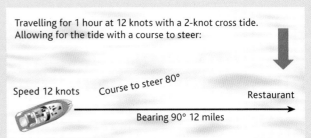

Travelling for 1 hour at 12 knots with a 2-knot cross tide. Allowing for the tide with a course to steer:

Speed 12 knots    Course to steer 80°

Restaurant

Bearing 90° 12 miles

By steering 10° into the tide we 'crab' down our bearing line and arrive at the restaurant in time for supper

▲ Diagram 2.

I have shown here how to be as accurate as possible, but I wouldn't bother with the 70%. I would use the full amount, which may mean you are overcompensating if the tide is not directly on the beam, but there is no harm in arriving a little uptide of your destination.

# ETIQUETTE

Be aware of wash and how it affects others. Always pass astern of any vessel you may be crossing or overtaking. Better still, keep far enough away from other vessels so that your wash does not affect them.

Or if the density of traffic is too great for this, do whatever it takes for your hull to reduce the wash it creates. This may well mean slowing down.

Give a wide berth to fishermen in their dories and day boats and, of course, if you spot the alpha flag. This means that they have a diver down, and you are required to keep clear and pass making as little wash as possible.

Other than that, a quick recap of the Rules of the Road, the Colregs or the International Regulations for the Prevention of Collisions at Sea (IRPCS).

Do remember that the term 'power-driven vessels' (defined by the Colregs as driven by machinery) covers motorboats and rowing boats. The machinery in the rowing boat is the oar and the rowlock. The machinery in the motorboat will be the gearbox and propeller. The difference between the two is that the effort in one is supplied by an engine and the effort in the other is supplied by a person. This is important because

▶ Alpha flag: diver down.

generally the Colregs refer to power giving way to sail, but actually within 'power' there are two categories. Here is the list of who gives way to whom:

| |
|---|
| **A boat under engine (power)**<br>Gives way to |
| **A rowing boat (power)**<br>Gives way to |
| **A sailing boat**<br>Gives way to |
| **A vessel fishing or trawling**<br>Gives way to |
| **A vessel constrained by draught, restricted in ability to manoeuvre or not under command.** |
| Any vessel overtaking keeps out of the way until past and clear. |

▲ The helm of this Sunseeker Camargue 50 has judged it to perfection: despite the fact that he is passing ahead of the four yachts, his wash has dissipated before they cross it.

## Is the other boat going ahead or astern?

Here's how to tell in a crossing situation if another vessel will go ahead of you or astern of you. Watch the background — as long as that is changing, you will miss the other boat. If it is eating up the background and spitting it out astern, the other boat will go ahead of you. If the background is opening out ahead of it and being eaten by its stern, you are going ahead of the other boat. If the background is static and you are closing, you are going to collide.

## Dinghy at night?

Under seven metres going at less than seven knots you are allowed to show a single all-round white light. In a dinghy this is usually just the torch you carry, but here is an idea: a cap light.

?

# 13 SAFETY AND MOB STRATEGY

*'If we look after our safety equipment, our safety equipment will look after us.'*

What safety equipment do you need? To a degree that depends where you will be sailing. It is worth contacting the Maritime Coastguard Agency to establish what they require a coded boat (that is to say, a boat that is for charter) to carry, if they are sailing in the same waters. Or check with the Environment Agency for inland waters.

## LIFEJACKETS

Is it a good idea to wear a lifejacket? Well, you tell me. I know I cannot breathe underwater. I've tried and it didn't work. I am also at an age and have lived such a splendid life that at any moment my body could decide that it has had enough. So I will fall to the water stroke-bound or heart stopped, incapable of helping myself. A lifejacket will keep me afloat. That is all it will do, but it is a start.

### ESSENTIAL SAFETY GEAR

My essentials would be:

**Lifejackets**: worth wearing.

**Throwing line**: the first thing you do if someone goes overboard is throw a floating line to him. If he can grab it you can drag him back to the boat.

**Lifebuoys**: that'll be the second thing to throw to an MOB.

**Lights on lifebuoys**: you need these at night and on overcast days.

**Lifesavers**: with these fitted into the jacket you can retrieve an unconscious person from the water. It also makes retrieving a conscious MOB that much easier.

**MOB retrieval rig/system**: you will need some system to get an MOB out, if he cannot help himself.

**DSC radio**: to call for help. A Mayday if a person or vessel is in grave and imminent danger and needs immediate assistance. A Pan Pan if the matter is urgent but not grave and imminent.

**EPIRB**: to signal a vessel's distress at sea.

**PLB**: to signal a person's distress at sea.

**AIS/DSC beacon**: carried by the casualty in the water (at sea), in the lifejacket, to signal to other vessels with AIS (Automatic Identification System) that there is a man in the water. This also alerts the mother ship, via DSC VHF radio, that a man is in the water. The AIS will give the coordinates of the MOB's position.

For my life to be saved I need the means for my retrieval back on board, stowed within my lifejacket. I need a Lifesaver. Then I need someone on the boat who has practised return to the man overboard and man overboard retrieval and who has a rig ready to go. Then I can be saved.

So, yes, I think it is a good idea to wear a lifejacket. All the professional sailors I know wear a lifejacket, even if they are using it as a harness to clip a lifeline to, whether they are at sea, on the river, in a canal or in a dinghy, especially in a dinghy. It's your call, of course.

Having decided that wearing a lifejacket is a good idea, you need to know that the jacket you are wearing is in date and in good condition so that it has a chance of inflating correctly and remaining inflated when you need it.

A few simple checks will assure you that the jacket should deploy correctly:

1 Open the jacket. A zip? Velcro?

2 Check the condition of the bladder. Any brown marks indicate possible weak areas which might become holes.

3 Are the retro reflective strips in place?

4 Is the gas cylinder clean or is it corroded? If it is corroded it should be disposed of. Has the corroded cylinder caused the bladder behind it to go brown?

5 If the cylinder is in good condition, is it screwed in tightly? If it is loose, the gas could simply expel outside the bladder and not inflate the jacket.

6 If the cylinder is clean and there is no hole in the end and it weighs what it says stamped on the side, then there is gas in it and it doesn't need changing. Safety companies will change them as a matter of course every five years. But there is no need if the cylinder is clean and weighs what it should weigh.

7 Check the firing head.

8 Check the webbing and crotch straps for wear.

9 Now with an in-date firing head and cylinder full of $CO_2$ back in place, inflate the jacket. There is much debate about this. I have always said that you should use a pump (a dinghy or bike one) so as not to introduce any moisture into the inside of the bladder. The technical department of a very well-known lifejacket manufacturer has told me that any moisture from breath makes no difference and they are concerned that if you use a pump you might overinflate the jacket. This is rather overcautious, as I am sure that anyone who is going to the trouble of looking at and servicing their jacket is not going to go mad pumping it up. You are pumping the jacket up until it's firm only to check that it will remain inflated for 24 hours. You decide which is best. Blowing up by mouth or pump, clearly both are acceptable. I'll stick with the pump. It is important to check that the jacket stays inflated for 24 hours, though.

▲ Amy Neilson, of Sailing Holidays, sporting a Seasafe MOB lifesavers jacket.

10 When you come to pack it away, expel all the air out of it by pressing the release valve in the oral inflation tube. Make sure the lanyard for the manual toggle is led correctly so the firing head will deploy correctly if you need to pull it. And then follow the fold lines of the jacket so that you repack it as it was packed by the manufacturer. If in doubt, check the internet for packing videos for your brand. Or if you are not sure, hand it to a safety expert and get them to do it.

## FIRING SYSTEMS

All brands of firing system rely on something dissolving. This releases a spring, which fires a pin through the end of the gas cylinder to allow the gas to inflate the jacket.

Well-known brands of firing system, in no particular order, are:

**UML (United Moulders Ltd):** has a soluble piece of paper in a cartridge. Cartridges have the expiry date written on them. If out of date it should be replaced.

**Halkey Roberts:** has a bobbin of microcrystalline cellulose that dissolves. Bobbins have the date of manufacture stamped on the side. If you are within six years of this, the bobbin is in date. They allow three years on the shelf and three years in service. If older than six years, the bobbin is out of date and should be replaced.

**Hammar hydrostatic:** has a unique hydrostatic valve that works by the pressure difference between the inside of the bladder and the outside. When the inflator is immersed in water by 10cm, the hydrostatic valve opens and water will have access to a water-sensitive element. This in turn releases a spring mechanism, which pierces the $CO_2$ cylinder. It can withstand spray, wave splash and high humidity without causing accidental inflation. So they say. Other jackets with soluble triggers could deploy if you were completely drenched by a wave. The expiry date is written on the inflator cap. It also has a red/green indicator. If the indicator is green but the cap is out of date, it needs to be

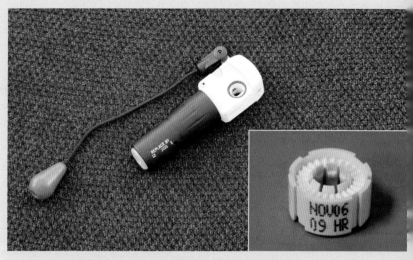

▲ UML head, expired in December 2015. (Inset) Halkey Roberts salt bobbin made on 6 November 2009, out of date since 5 November 2015.

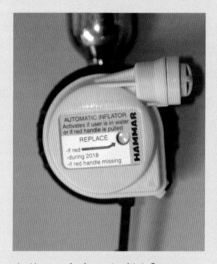

▲ Hammar hydrostatic: this inflator cap, although not fired because it shows green, runs out of date in 2018.

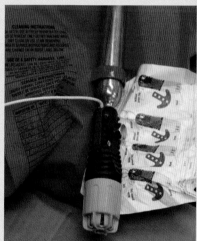

▲ Lalizas firing head, which has a pill.

replaced, and if the indicator is red, the cap needs to be replaced because it has been fired.

With Hammar heads the cylinder is inside the jacket. Care must be taken to check the cylinder is not corroded and that it is screwed in tightly. Some service companies glue these in to make

sure they couldn't come out, as they are not as easy to access as a cylinder that is on the outside.

Some lifejacket brands have their own firing head system which will be activated by a disolving bobbin or a pill. Examples are Secumar and Lalizas, which both have a pill that dissolves.

## Some lifejacket brands and the firing heads they use

Baltic: UML

Besto: UML

Crewsaver: Hammar and UML

ISP: UML

Lalizas: its own system with Hammar and bobbins

Mullion: UML

Mustang: Hammar and bobbin

Ocean Safety: Hammar and UML

Seasafe: UML

Secumar: secumatic firing head activated by a dissolving pill

Spinlock: Hammar and UML

Typhoon: Halkey Roberts bobbin

I don't like relying on outside people where my lifejacket is concerned. It's rather like packing one's own parachute. While safety service companies will be very good I am sure, I have also heard and witnessed some horror stories. I was handed what I was told were two brand-new jackets bought at a boat show. I was to fit Lifesavers to them. One jacket had a Halkey Roberts firing head that had been fired. The other jacket had an in-date, unfired firing head (hooray), but the gas cylinder had a hole in the end and had no gas in it. Neither automatic jacket would have worked and yet they were brand new. Someone deserves to be shot for that sort of thing.

Cylinders and firing heads can get swapped around in shops and at shows, so as soon as you have bought a new jacket, check in the shop that the firing head is in date and that the cylinder is in good condition and has not been fired. Or once you have agreed to buy it, get the sales staff to do it for you. It saves a lot of hassle later on.

 Scan this QR code to watch a demonstration of how to service a lifejacket:

## What do lifejackets with windows and indicators tell you?

You will see some lifejackets that have a window so you can see the state of the firing head. They have a code on the outside that shows two greens = all OK. Either indicator red = a problem. I have discovered that sailors are confused by this. They think that two greens means that everything is OK inside the lifejacket. It does not mean this at all. Two greens means that the gas cylinder is screwed in tightly and that the head has not been fired manually or automatically. It does not tell you anything about the condition of the cylinder or the expiry date of the trigger for the firing head or the condition of the bladder. Two greens or no two greens, you need to look inside the jacket and check that all is well and that the firing cartridge is in date.

Two greens means the gas cylinder is screwed in, that the seal for the cylinder is intact, that there is no hole in the end of it and that the jacket has not been fired either automatically or manually.

## Crotch straps

Lifejackets are fitted with crotch or thigh straps. The thought is that you adjust the jackets to be comfortable to wear and perhaps therefore a little looser than they should be. The straps are to stop the casualty slipping out of the jacket if they are being lifted out vertically and they are unconscious. And that makes sense.

But I have found that occasionally I get my crotch strap caught round something. The other day it was on the locking nut for the gypsy on the windlass. As I stood up I was caught off balance for a moment. A friend had a similar experience, but more worryingly he nearly fell overboard. So, as with everything, wearing crotch or thigh straps may be a context thing. The choice would be to wear the lifejacket a little tighter and not do up the straps, or to have the jacket adjusted for comfort and do up the straps, which should be as tight as bearable to avoid catching on anything.

# MAN OVERBOARD

One of the key concerns is what would happen if a man went overboard. How would you get them back on board? All strategies and systems that you read about assume that the man can help himself. What if he can't? What are you going to do then?

## Return to the MOB

First you need to get the boat back to him. If you are at sea there are a number of turns you can make, depending on the type of vessel, but the one that makes sense for leisure boats is the Williamson turn.

### Williamson turn

As soon as the man has gone overboard, note your heading, then, maintaining your speed, put the helm hard over and make a 60° alteration of course in either direction, port or starboard. As soon as you are on this new course, put the helm hard over in the other direction until you are sailing the reciprocal of your original course, effectively motoring back down your wake. You will find the man in here, somewhere.

For a motorboat planing at 25 knots this amounts to: man overboard, note heading, helm 60° to port, count steadily to 5 (...1...2...3...4...5...), then helm hard astarboard and come round to the reciprocal of your original heading. You should now be travelling back down your own wake.

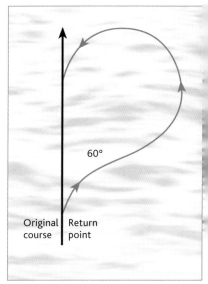

▶ Williamson turn.

▶ Throwing line at the ready.

You will always want to approach upwind of the MOB. You must be very careful not to have the propellers turning when he is alongside and abaft the beam.

Now throw him the floating line. If he grabs this, you can haul him towards the boat and he may be able to climb up the bathing ladder, if the boat has one.

What if he does not respond to the throwing line? Perhaps he is unconscious, in shock or hypothermic? And what if you are the only person on the boat?

Getting him out is not going to be easy.

## MOB Lifesavers

If the casualty is wearing a lifejacket with an MOB Lifesaver inside and you have prepared and practised and have a retrieval rig ready to set, it may be possible.

I have spent a great deal of time working out how to get a man out of the drink if he cannot help himself and I have concluded that the MOB has to have the means of his retrieval back on board contained within his lifejacket. Much of the time you cannot reach down to him to attach a line. Even off a bathing platform it is not easy to attach anything to a lifejacket.

That is why I came up with MOB Lifesavers (www.moblifesavers.com).

A Lifesaver is a three-metre length of incredibly strong floating rope that is hand spliced into a loop. A triangle is formed at one end, and the other end is attached to the lifting becket in the lifejacket.

And that is the first thing that takes sailors by surprise. They automatically assume that you attach any line for retrieving a man from the drink to the 'D' ring on the lifejacket if there is one. No, because that is not what it's for and the rescuer cannot get to it when the lifejacket is inflated. The lifting becket is what you are to lift the man out with. Mind you, of course you'll attach whatever you have to whatever you can on a lifejacket to get the man out. The Lifesaver is incredibly strong and will lift a Mini motor car with four adults inside.

It is coiled up on top of the bladder in the lifejacket and the jacket is closed. When the lifejacket deploys the Lifesaver floats out on to the water and you can grab it with the boathook and attach the man to the boat. So that's part one of the exercise, the man is now attached to the boat.

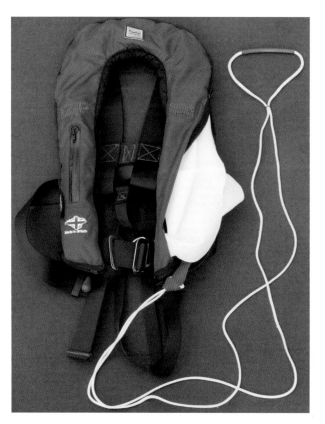

▲ A Lifesaver is a three-metre length of HMPE rope that's spliced into a loop, with a triangle formed in one end.

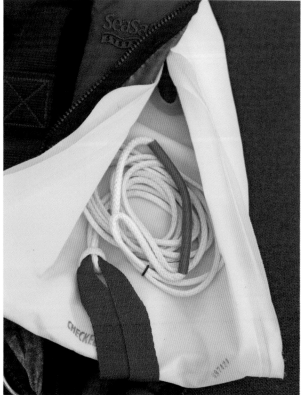

▲ The other end is attached to the lifting becket in the lifejacket, and the Lifesaver is coiled on top of the bladder.

## MOB LIFESAVER

▲ The MOB goes in and the lifejacket deploys.

▲ The lifesaver floats out on to the water.

▲ The lifesaver is grabbed with the boathook…

▲ …and…

▲ the MOB is attached to the boat.

▲ 'Nigel' – resting.

◀ Here we have been able to use the motorised passarelle. We have added in a strop to bring the MOB out horizontally. This is also much more comfortable. I know. I make a very good unresponsive and unhelpful man overboard.

## Retrieval

Part two, retrieval on board, depends on the type of boat you have. Motorboats do not have lifting means like sailing boats, such as halyards, nor do they generally have much by way of height.

Some of the bigger boats have cranes, some have electric passerelles and these can all be pressed into service and will get the man out. Davits generally are not so helpful as they are outboard and once you have raised the man out of the water, it is difficult to swing him inboard. They also do not generally have sufficient height to get a man on board. But recovery is all about seeing what you have available and what will work on your boat.

Remember in all this that it is very likely the bigger person of any partnership who has fallen in and it is down to the smaller, more slight, less strong person of the two to get the other one out. This is something I bear in mind always and the systems I propose can be handled by a 7-stone girl and provide gearing for her to get a 17-stone man out of the water and back on board.

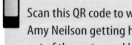 Scan this QR code to watch a video of Amy Neilson getting her father Barrie out of the water and back on board:

## Getting an unconscious man out of the water and retrieved back on board

We have looked at this for all types of motorboat. We use 'Nigel', our man-overboard mannequin. And they don't come more unconscious than Nigel. He does nothing to help himself at all. Nigel's means of rescue, his Lifesaver, is contained within his lifejacket.

Now you need to establish just how you would get a man back on board.

Motorboats are generally fairly stable at the stern in any sea because their weight (heavy engines) is aft and the stern tends not to bounce up and down too much. Whereas if there is any wave motion the stern of a sailing boat could be moving about dangerously and you would want to bring an MOB back in amidships.

But what motorboats don't generally have are lifting means or height. Some have cranes for lifting RIBs and Jetskis on board. Others have motorised passerelles, which can be used as a crane. Some have bathing platforms that can be lowered. Some also have height above the water (a flybridge, an aft poop deck, a wheelhouse) from which you might suspend a tackle to lift the man out. If you have sufficient height, attach your lifting means to the Lifesaver. If not, attach it to the lifting becket directly.

If you are using a tackle, or 'Handy Billy' as it is called, it is important to have the best, with ratcheted

## EXAMPLE OF AN MOB RETRIEVAL

Here Simon has applied his mind to the business of getting a man out and on to the bathing platform of his Doral Boca Grande. He has bought a strop and a ratchet winch and has slung this affair between two stern cleats.

▶ Here Simon does not have any height, so he has adapted a ratchet system and slung it across the stern of the boat to bring the man out over the bathing platform. Note how he is wearing a safety line.

 Scan the QR code to watch a video on retrieving a man back on board:

## MOB RETRIEVAL TO A RIB OR OVER A SPONSON

If the MOB is able to stand on the cavitation plate of the outboard, you can raise the outboard and bring him back on board.

▲ Circled is the cavitation plate. Raise the engine to get the MOB back on board. Engine off.

For the retrieval of a dead weight over a sponson, you need two lifting beckets ideally, or two people, one on each arm.

blocks and the finest line, so you minimise the amount of friction in the system. I have been working with Harken and recommend its six-part tackle, which will enable a small person to haul a large person out of the drink. A six-part tackle reduces a 12-stone weight to just a few stone. I can lift myself with the Harken six-part tackle and I weigh rather more than 12 stone. In fact, I weigh so much these days that I refer to my weight in kilos. That way no one has any idea what I weigh – well, in the UK anyway, where we deal in stones, and in America, where they deal in pounds.

The point is that you need to be prepared and think about how you would do it on your boat. What might work? The key to all of this is having a Lifesaver in the lifejacket. Without that, none of the above will work.

It's not going to look pretty, but if you have a man in the water and need to get him out, these will be exceptional circumstances and you won't be too fussed about what is pretty. You will want something that is effective.

## OPTIONS FOR LIFTING AN UNCONSCIOUS MAN OUT

▲ A bathing platform that can be lowered under the MOB...

▶ and raised to bring him out of the water.

▶ There would be enough height if you slung a tackle from the radar arch.

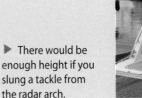

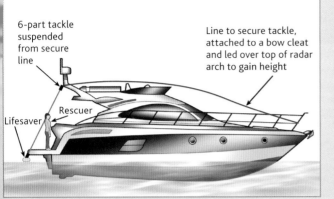

MOB retrieval rig – using radar arch to gain height

6-part tackle suspended from secure line

Line to secure tackle, attached to a bow cleat and led over top of radar arch to gain height

Rescuer

Lifesaver

◄ You would lead a line from the bow up to the radar arch and sling a six-part tackle from here.

▶ Here the six-part tackle is suspended from a line off the flybridge.

Crane

◄ These chaps have got height from which you could sling your six-part tackle.

▶ This chap has a crane for lifting the MOB out of the water.

▶ Six-part tackle suspended from a line across the coachroof, with a strop under the knees to bring 'Nigel' out horizontally.

▶▶ Six-part tackle suspended from superstructure off a line led from the bow (inset).

## MOB RETRIEVAL RIG SET UP ON A BARGE

▲ First, run a line across the wheelhouse roof from one side…

▲ Hang the six-part tackle from this line.

▼ to the other.

▲ Use carabiners that are easy to open and close. A screw lock carabiner has been added here. This will not open accidentally, nor will the carabiner above it in this shot. Notice the 'mousing' of the shackle to stop the pin coming out.

▲ The Harken six-part tackle.

### Why do we shiver?

We shiver because the skin has become too cool and has sent a signal to the brain that we need to warm up. The brain then starts the muscles expanding and contracting, and this twitching effect produces heat.

## Horizontal vs. vertical lift

The important thing to consider is the casualty's condition. He may be hypothermic. This could very well be why he is unable to help himself. His fingers may not be working properly.

As the body temperature drops, the body conserves warm blood at the core for the organs, and the blood to the extremities is reduced. The result is that you lose the use of your fingers and toes.

In addition to this, the body experiences hydrostatic squeeze. The pressure of the water keeps warm blood flowing into the centre of the body. When the MOB is lifted out of the water this pressure disappears, and if he is lifted vertically the blood can rush away from the heart to the legs, causing a massive heart attack.

If you bring the man out horizontally this does not happen. Use a strop to go under the legs and clip it into the carabiner of the lifting tackle along with the Lifesaver. As a matter of interest and from experience, it is much more comfortable to be lifted out horizontally. When I have been lifted by just my Lifesaver attached to the lifting becket, I have sometimes experienced quite a 'grip' around the nether regions from the crotch strap. Nice to know it is working though, I suppose.

## Temperature and the body

The table shows what happens to the human body at various temperatures. Interestingly, because they do not have any warm water currents running through them, average temperatures in UK rivers are generally a couple of degrees less than the sea.

| Temperature  and the body | |
|---|---|
| Normal body temperature | 98.6°F (37°C) |
| Hypothermia sets in | 95°F (35°C) |
| Mental capacity lost | 93°F (33.9°C) |
| Unconscious | 86°F (30°C) |
| Dead | 80°F (26.7°C) |
| Cold water definition | <25°C |
| UK sea water temperature minimum (February) | 5°C |

# 14 SEASICKNESS

Seasickness, or *mal de mer*, is just as unpleasant and debilitating whichever language you choose. It is no measure of the man or woman either. Nelson, our greatest admiral, suffered from seasickness, and seasickness is likely to affect all of us at some point. You may just feel slightly disorientated or be physically sick and completely incapacitated. Seasickness is the only thing that would cause a man to give up all his worldly possessions to be free from.

And the only real answer to seasickness is to return to land. But that in itself may not provide instant relief once seasickness has set in. I have known people who, 48 hours after having returned to dry land after only a few hours in a very gentle sea, were still paralysed by the imbalance in their bodies and physically sick. Some bodies will adapt to the motion at sea and the seasickness will reduce after a couple of days. Others never adapt and will be seasick as long as they are in that environment.

## WHAT IS SEASICKNESS?

Seasickness is motion sickness, just like car sickness, air sickness, train sickness or the sickness you get on fairground rides. You can even get it while playing fast-moving computer games or watching films that cut quickly from one scene to the next. And it is caused by a conflict between your brain and the body's vestibular system (a network of channels, nerves and fluids in the inner ear which gives the brain its sense of balance and motion).

On a rocking boat the eyes tell the brain that everything is still, because your eyeline is still relative to the boat, but your body's vestibular system tells the brain that you are rocking, moving. This is especially so if you are down belowdecks where your eyes cannot catch glimpses of the horizon. There is a mismatch between these two systems and your brain cannot update the information and it becomes confused, which leads to nausea and vomiting.

The signs that motion sickness is coming on are: cold sweats, going pale, dizziness, an increase in saliva and eventually vomiting. Additionally, you might also experience rapid, shallow breathing, headaches and extreme drowsiness.

People most likely to suffer from seasickness are pregnant women and those who suffer from migraines. Young children can also suffer from motion sickness but tend to grow out of it.

Other factors that make you more likely to suffer seasickness include a person's fear or anxiety about travelling (sailing in this instance), poor ventilation and an inability to see out of a window to help with orientation.

## PREVENTATIVE MEASURES

What can you do to prevent or reduce seasickness?

### Practically

**1** Try to stay calm.

**2** Try relaxing. Music on headphones can help.

**3** Come up on deck in the fresh air. This will also allow you to see the horizon, which may help. If you are feeling seasick you need to be wrapped up warmly when on deck. You don't need to start getting cold, and if you are feeling seasick you will not want to move. You need to be wearing a lifejacket and be tethered to the boat. When you are seasick you will not care about anything other than your seasickness. You might even feel that being in the cool inviting water might be preferable to the misery you are suffering, so a lifeline is vital.

4 Try to keep away from diesel fumes.

5 Try to avoid rich and fatty foods before setting sail and on passage.

## Medically

There are tablets you can take before setting sail, which fall into two categories. I have listed only a few brands here; there are others.

### 1. Antihistamines

Tablets: Stugeron is a well-known brand. You take a tablet two hours before travel and then once every eight hours for an adult. Read the information on the leaflet in the packet.

### 2. Hyoscine

Tablets: Kwells is a well-known brand. You take a tablet 30 minutes before travelling and then take one every six hours but no more than three tablets in 24 hours. Read the information on the leaflet in the packet.

▲ Ginger biscuits and root ginger.

Patches: Scopoderm is the well-known brand here. You place one patch behind one ear about five or six hours prior to travelling. A patch lasts for up to three days (72 hours). Read the information on the leaflet in the packet.

Be aware that all antihistamine and hyoscine medications can cause drowsiness.

## Complementary therapies

### Ginger

Ginger biscuits, ginger tea and root ginger may all help to prevent seasickness. There is no definitive scientific evidence to support this, but it is amazing what the power of 'belief' can achieve, and ginger has long been considered to be an effective answer by sailors. I have ginger biscuits on board at all times, mostly because I like them a lot but also because you never know. My crew will always have a cup of tea and a ginger biscuit. And we get very little seasickness. Coincidence?

### Pâté Hénaff

Monsieur Hénaff, a Breton, came up with the idea of compressing an entire pig, bones, trotters and all, into a tin as food for the poor. Not only is it cheap and nutritious, it also has magical properties apparently. It prevents seasickness. French sailors and fishermen swear by it. It is surprisingly tasty.

### Acupressure bands

These are elasticated bands that are worn around the wrists with a button that presses on a 'pressure' point on the inside of your wrist. Again, there is little or no scientific evidence to support their efficacy in preventing seasickness, but many people swear by them.

▲ Acupressure bands.

## Boarding ring glasses

These are glasses that have a subliminal horizon in the lenses, both ahead and peripherally. This apparently prevents seasickness. The advertising says that they were tested by the French navy and were successful in 95% of cases, but, of course, any results are a French national secret! Hearsay evidence of efficacy is patchy. You put them on only when you start to feel seasick. A friend of mine tested them and did not find that they made much difference. I have heard that one woman who suffered badly from seasickness found that they helped when she went below to make a meal or log entries. Where before this was impossible, wearing the glasses she was able to do this.

The thinking behind them is spot on. If you lose sight of the horizon as you go below, the conflict starts between your brain and your vestibular system (the inner ear). By putting on the glasses you give your eyes a horizon, a local horizon, and your eyes/brain and inner ear read the same information, which removes the conflict.

Another way you can help to reduce seasickness is by being careful what you eat prior to departure or on passage. Large, fatty meals are not ideal. That said, being at sea is tiring work. For a start, the body is permanently on the move as you try to balance against the motion of the boat. So you will get hungry and substantial food will be required. If you have become 'overly refreshed' the night before a passage, you may not be feeling quite the ticket, regardless of setting sail.

Try to relax and be involved with the business of sailing or navigation. There can be nothing worse than

▲ It's not a great look, but if they work, who cares, and you wear them for only a short time, just when you are feeling sick.

sitting there feeling dreadful and not knowing how long this misery will last because the skipper has not told anyone when they expect to reach port. I think being involved and part of the decision-making process of the passage or trip helps to keep seasickness at bay.

Then, of course, the motion of the boat can be changed. If you are slamming into a sea it is not going to be comfortable. If you went about and ran with the sea, the motion would be much more comfortable. These are things to take into consideration when you plan your trips, to make sure that you give your crew the most comfortable ride possible.

Finally on seasickness, you will become dehydrated very quickly, so it is important to drink lots of water.

# 15 EPILOGUE

As I have said throughout, preparation is the key to success in any of this. Figuring out in advance how you can make things easier, having a system in place for whatever manoeuvre you are about to undertake, with lines of the right length and everything to hand, will ensure things go smoothly.

And, of course, practising. I know you have very little time available for your boating, but practising manoeuvres and techniques is important.

It's also worth considering how you would get a man in the water back on board. Set up a retrieval rig or system and check it out. Should an emergency arise, you will be ready for it.

There is fabulous fun to be had on the water, wherever you are. So I hope you find the techniques and tips in this book useful, and that they lead to stress-free motorboating that everyone can share and enjoy.

# INDEX